DAWN OF A NEW FEELING

Dawn of a New Feeling

The Neocontemplative Condition

RAFFAELE MILANI

Translated by Corrado Federici

McGill-Queen's University Press
Montreal & Kingston · London · Chicago

ISBN 978-0-2280-1096-8 (cloth)
ISBN 978-0-2280-1321-1 (ePDF)
ISBN 978-0-2280-1322-8 (ePUB)

Legal deposit second quarter 2022
Bibliothèque nationale du Québec

Printed in Canada on acid-free paper that is 100% ancient forest free (100% post-consumer recycled), processed chlorine free

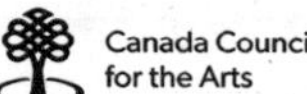

We acknowledge the support of the Canada Council for the Arts.

Nous remercions le Conseil des arts du Canada de son soutien.

Library and Archives Canada Cataloguing in Publication

Title: Dawn of a new feeling: the neocontemplative condition/
  Raffaele Milani; translated by Corrado Federici.

Other titles: Albe di un nuovo sentire. English | Neocontemplative condition

Names: Milani, Raffaele, author. | Federici, Corrado, 1946– translator.

Description: Translation of: Albe di un nuovo sentire: la condizione
  neocontemplativa. | Includes bibliographical references and index.

Identifiers: Canadiana (print) 20210383208 | Canadiana (ebook)
  2021038333X | ISBN 9780228010968 (cloth) |
  ISBN 9780228013211 (ePDF) | ISBN 9780228013228 (ePUB)

Subjects: LCSH: Aesthetics. | LCSH: Art—Philosophy.

Classification: LCC BH39 .M516513 2022 | DDC 111/.85—dc23

This book was typeset by Marquis Interscript in 11/14 Sabon.

for Laura

Contents

and at the touch of love everyone becomes a poet
even though he had no Muse in him before

Plato, Symposium

Introduction

Architecture should be more than practical; it must also speak
to the heart. It represents the quest to find a spiritual home.
Only by thinking in these terms can we create a second Nature.

Emilio Ambasz

Let us cross the threshold and observe: The threads of the modern
and the postmodern are interconnected with digital-virtual reality forming a seemingly impermeable mesh that encircles us in
concrete and visible terms. Interior and exterior dimensions are
marked by signposts that compel us to remain within the bounds
of a new linguistic and anthropological chaos where art appears
to have lost its meaning. Let us, then, go "outside" and try to see
the world without the filters of the new technologies or the
simulations of the avant-garde and the various "isms" of more
than a century.

In the era of the new virtuality and globalization, there are
two important interpretive frames for evaluating aesthetics and
art that we have before us: on the one hand, at the limits of
imitation, there is postmodernism, characterized by quotation
and ornamentation, and, on the other, there is realism, which
strives for authenticity in its pursuit of depicting the object as
object. In the context of creative experience and thought in
which these frames materialize, it is important to reconsider the
aura of contemplation through the writings of Karl Jaspers,
Giorgio Colli, Luigi Pareyson, Rosario Assunto, and Elémire
Zolla. What, then, is the nature of seeing and imagining, we
might ask ourselves, taking into account as well the studies of

Erwin Panofsky, Aby Warburg, and Wolfgang Köhler? The search for the answer to this question takes the form of a broad perspective that leads us to the dawn of a new feeling.

Promptings that evoke treasured memories of the distant past and the classical world can be found in masterpieces of compelling intent that convey powerful visions but that have been abandoned in the course of time. From painting to architecture, from literature to sculpture, and from theatre to cinema, we have a mosaic of traces that constitute a turning point, an invitation to rediscover the capacity for a form of representation that does not rely on the strategies of shock, improvisation, and kitsch. Solitary figures in the arts – in music, from Olivier Messiaen to György Ligeti, from minimalist composers like Steve Reich to Michael Nyman; in the figurative arts, from Giorgio Morandi and Francis Bacon to Bill Viola, Anselm Kiefer, and Olafur Eliasson; in cinema, from Luchino Visconti to Andrei Tarkovsky and Lech Majewsky; in dance and theatre, from Jean Cocteau and Martha Graham to Peter Brook, Tadeus Kantor, and Eimuntas Necrosius – enable voices and images to form a great expressive wave. With this new mode of feeling, which also involves absorbed recollection, a previously unknown and vivid relationship with landscape, garden, and other aspects of nature is experienced by many citizens who do not want to be excluded from the *poiesis* of the green expanses. It is not a matter of valorizing only famous architects but all people who share a common creativity: the winds of aesthetics and environmental art. Along with this, we see the growing importance of silence and slowness in the making of art, which involves direct and indirect reliance on traditional techniques. At the same time, we see a return of the lessons learned from antiquity that serve as guiding principles as we move into the future.

Contrary to what Jaron Lanier thinks, artificial intelligence does not seem to invite us to think deeply, to plumb the depths of the heart and the human spirit. Starting and maintaining a flower or vegetable garden – like maintaining a library – is a way of improving the world. Reading and contemplation are fundamental activities for combatting mental atrophy in today's world.

The internet and artificial intelligence have contributed to an increase in diagnosed attention disorders, including a significant loss in the ability to concentrate and to intuit.

We therefore should rethink myth and antiquity for the future and liberate ourselves from the things that imprison us: Let us look to "the outdoors." Let us reread Hermann Broch's *The Death of Virgil*, Marguerite Yourcenar's *Memoirs of Hadrian*, or Christa Wolf's *Cassandra*, and through these works we may overcome the improvisation we see all around us.

It is not a matter of dismissing the twentieth century by highlighting only a few uncommon aspects or sources of tradition, but rather rediscovering hidden or forgotten connective strands, or locating in the recent works of authors traces of a past that still survive in the age of globalization and the new virtuality. A relationship with the experience of feeling and living in an aesthetics of understanding, of allowing the stream of aesthetic aura and catharsis to flow once again. Here, I am attempting to suggest a pathway for escaping the torments and provocations that for more than a century have provided space for the pleasures of the repulsive and the offensive, as well as for magical or illusory-technical media-driven products. When confronted with the process of "reproducing" the visible world, I propose that the way to proceed is by highlighting the ingenious creations of minds inspired by myth, culture, and history: in a word, harmony.

Allowing ourselves to be inspired by a syncretism of arts and crafts, forms of knowledge, rituals, and representations, such as that obtained during the Florentine and Roman Renaissance, stands as a way of crossing that threshold and entering an eclectic and illuminating realm that offers us a new appreciation for the eye that does not see things but *forms of things* that signify other things. Attention to silence, slowness, mindfulness of the classical world, and new ideas concerning nature and the ecology are taking root against the power of computing technology, which is by now the expression of a new kind of global enslavement.

Let us return to thinking about the wisdom of the ancients; let us recover the silence of the Muse Polyhymnia. As Monica Centanni (2006) reminds us, in 404 CE, a fire in Constantinople destroyed the statues that Constantine had dedicated to the Muses in the senate chamber in Byzantium, a sad omen of their decline and disappearance, as the Greek historian Zosimus would declare a century later: the threat of *amousia* (without harmony) looming over the world. We have the last reference to the Muses in ancient Greek poetry a few decades earlier in the fifth book of the *Dionysiaca*. Nonnus of Panopolis recounts the arrival of the gods at the wedding feast of Cadmus and Harmonia, with Ares, who extends an empty hand to Aphrodite and dances naked for the wedding of his daughter. Apollo enters accompanied by the nine Muses; the only one of them mentioned by name is Polyhymnia, the Muse of dance and sacred song, as she moves her fingers in eloquent gestures and her hands in lovely forms that communicate a silent wisdom. In book 9 of the *Anthologia Palatina* (Palatine anthology), the nine deities appear and pronounce their names, but the last of them, Polyhymnia, without uttering her name and enveloped by her robes, states (in the final hexameter couplet): "I do not speak; I express myself only with the palm of my hand that enchants the heart: my eloquent silence speaks through the gesture." Polyhymnia, an iteration of the philosophical impulse, radiates a solitary and melancholy light into the minds of artists and poets, inspiring them and enflaming them with masterly images. Centanni writes, "But what special obsession inspires Polyhymnia the philosopher-poetess? What does Polyhymnia think and know? Does she contemplate the secret of wisdom, the musical harmony of the cosmos taught to the Sirens by the Muses? Does she contemplate knowledge of the mystery – the riddle that Oedipus believed he could easily solve – the tragic riddle of the Sphinx that was taught to her by the Muses? Does she know the wisdom of the past and the future with which the Sybil was raised?" (158; translated by Corrado Federici). Polyhymnia knows and sees all of this at a glance. The dream sees harmony and harmony sees the dream. The principle containing both dream and harmony is the art of contemplation, the supreme capacity for surpassing the visible in order to access conscious and unconscious images of representation.

Through this narrative, we can recapture that ancient, enigmatic act of remaining quiet as well as that silent dancing with eyes turned toward the future as we meditate on the dawning of a new day.

I

The Neocontemplative Condition

**1 TOWARD A PHILOSOPHY
OF REPRESENTATION**

The presence of the theme of love of philosophy seems natural in a work that deals with feeling; yet it is a good idea to underline its importance in the face of a disconcerting lack of interest in this idea, which we witness today in the reorganization of academic programs and universities (and the media system), with drastic cancellations and substitutions of courses and programs. And it seems important to do so starting with a philosophy of representation, that is, an aesthetic vision of the "quality" of life, the power of the imaginative mind, and the dynamic system of the emotions.

Speaking of the philosophical conception of the good, Gianni Carchia writes:

> Philosophy's constant yearning for truth quiets and relaxes in the spontaneous appearance of an always renewed line that inscribes being, leading it toward meaning and giving it form. The entire truth of *legein* (logos), therefore, lies in this art of connecting, unifying, or selecting, or the art of signifying that precedes all predication and that indeed qualifies philosophy as a true musical art, if what Theodore Adorno said about music is true, i.e., that it is "the logical synthesis that does not judge." (Carchia 2000, 34; translated by Corrado Federici)

And this is, perhaps, close to the ultimate meaning we can ascribe to the interconnections between philosophy and poetry, which reveal the depth of a dimension in which we no longer perceive a background or a form.

> In the depth of chiasmus, essence reveals itself as appearance, but appearance, in turn, draws its light and meaning from essence. Figures and the beautiful direct us to that backdrop, without which they could not reveal themselves. Form discloses the background, which illuminates the form. Enigmatic and intricate arrangements of folds and envelopments are where the chiasmus resolves itself. Thomas Aquinas said as much in a concise and sublime manner in his *Commentary on Aristotle's "Metaphysics"*: "The reason why the philosopher is compared to the poet is that both are concerned with wonders." (Carchia, 35)

The 1980s and 1990s witnessed the genesis and spread of postmodernism, along with a new virtual representation of the sensible world; we might wonder, then, if it is not possible to talk of the emergence of a neocontemplative condition. This would not be, however, a gift from the digital information-technology world, as one might imagine at first blush. That would be confirming a deception because this virtuality has, in fact, perverted the spirit of contemplation; it has falsified authentic contact with nature, or at the very least it has separated feeling from the illusory power of technical devices. This union of perception and illusion was, nonetheless, historically necessary for the evolution of the representational mind, from cave paintings to the birth of myth. John Boardman (2004) gives an account of the way the ancient Greeks were able to reinvent the past, that is to say, how they recreated their past through images and objects. Boardman studies memory as an instrument of art. Today, what we feel we have lost is precisely this process of representing the past, a process that continued up until a few decades ago in Western culture. If there is nostalgia, it takes the form of a rediscovery and not a loss. We need to recover what virtual technology tends to erase.

The rediscovery of a deep symbolic feeling, like that engendered by the image of antiquity, does not necessarily entail the struggle to recover an earlier, distant world, as in Hans Sedlmayr's interpretation in *Art in Crisis: The Lost Center* (1983). Such would be an impossible project. And it is not at all obvious that we are suffering from, to use Zygmunt Bauman's term (2017), "retrotopia." The term refers a return to the past and a loss of confidence in a future based on the idea of progress and development. The author prefers to see the past as a place where we can find great hope for the future. What we can see or what we would like to see in terms of traces is a tangible indicator of a memory that continues to be operative, a memory characterized by the aura of a gaze that is transformed into contemplation as it transitions from the visible to the invisible and from the invisible to the visible. In this vein, important works by Viola, Messiaen, and Ligeti, alongside Igor Mitoraj, Francis Poulenc, Mario Luzi, Cristina Campo, Carlo Betocchi, and Andrea Zanzotto, can serve as signposts.

But what I would like to underscore here is the link between representation and expression in a powerful image that allows us to return to the roots of contemplation and, in turn, to the origin of the aesthetic act and the artistic act.

Giorgio Colli (1969) claims that every form of knowledge consists in memories, objects, and words that belong to the past. This is how a subject represents something to itself, even with a past where that something was not yet configured as something meaningful. In this way, using the German term *Vorstellung* (a mental image produced by prior perception of an object), modern philosophy situates us in relation to this making the past thing or event reappear before our eyes; it is re-evocation. The emphasis would, therefore, be on the representational function, which implies working through memory and time (Colli, 6; translated by Corrado Federici). Defining representation opens up a vast field: "The most intimate sentiment, Goethe's moment or Plotinus's ecstasy, is already a representation, as is the most abstract and universal thought" (Colli, 9). The world we see, touch, and think about is a representation, as is affirmed from the Upanishads to Parmenides. The world is a representation in that it is dependent on relationships determined by the fluctuating, unstable interaction between subject and object. At times, it is substance understood as a category or as a foundational element in philosophical terms; at other times, it is something immediate, not removed from sense perception. In saying this Colli reflects on the "enjoyment" of contemplators who either intuit or are moved by pathos, as when it seems to them that the world in which they live is an apparition or a veiled dream-like representation. This perception is also an intense and lasting experience for the individual contemplator, and it is also one that we have known for about three thousand years. Colli writes, "The individual who feels this pathos tends toward contemplation because to intuit is to contemplate and to contemplate is to withdraw oneself from the depths of life. Those who are immersed in this cannot feel its illusoriness. To know is to lose something from the well of life" (10). But we must add that the enjoyment of the moment, paradoxically, is more intense in the knower by reason of the fact that the instant glimpse of a fragment of life is unsettling to those who wisely detach themselves from life, suppressing their impulse to vanish into the image they know to be illusory. The world of things, which can be summed up in the term *life*, is like the dream of a god; in Greece this view was represented by the primitive Orphic figure of Phanes, something profound or hidden. The world of representation in which we find ourselves, both the world of life and the world of things and their images, form a chain or a system of relationships. Contemplation is nourished by the juxtaposition of representations while distinctions among meaning, imagination, intellect, and reason disappear in this state. Avoiding solipsism, an ever-present risk, the contemplator pierces the delirium of appearances, the web of representations, which are always evanescent, and becomes a performer in a play without an audience. Colli goes on to argue:

This is what comprises nature: the sky, the stars with their presumed laws, and humanity and its history, along with their loftiest thoughts and most significant actions. All this is nothing more than representation and we can only interpret it as a given of knowledge. All other words that human reason can invent as it presumes to unveil something substantial, elemental, and unifying with respect to the kaleidoscope of experience, words such as idea, spirit, will, instinct, action, and power, do not justify or explain anything. They merely reveal the intrusion of metaphysical concepts in the act of interpreting the driving nexus that representation as such already possesses, without transcendent or transcendental aid. (121)

Whether it points to something unknown or corresponds to something other than itself, representation produces a cluster of expressive chains in continuous expansion through the endlessly converging and diverging pathways of human activity, starting with language as constitutive of categories in a multiplicative image of the object. Therefore, to give expression to something in the necessity and randomness that rule our lives means to externalize immediacy through a series of representations that follow one another as though they were generated by an intricate caprice or playfulness. Art is the product of this process. More specifically, it is the expression of an expression, not so much and not only the expression of an object. At times, a representation that corresponds perfectly to the expression that inspires it cannot be found because it is elusive; it is naturally evanescent in that it causes both the subject and the object of the reference to vanish. We are amazed; dumbfounded we contemplate. Artistic representation is ungraspable; we can see this especially in music. And if we were capable of discerning an expression that corresponds to artistic representation, we would find it difficult to retrace the route taken to arrive at that point and we would nonetheless be in the thrall of something inexpressible. Whether abstract or concrete, art is an expression that exists alongside natural expressions. As they create, artists show us that there are, in everyday life, occasions for representation and evocation. Natural expressions adhere to concrete reality, whereas artistic expressions are elements that we could call the endpoint of an aesthetic process that also includes abstraction.

2 SALIENT FEATURES OF VIRTUAL REALITY

In the early 1990s Elémire Zolla and Tomás Maldonado were mistaken, for different reasons and using different approaches, in their assessment of the interrelationships between aesthetics, art, and nature in a society where, at the time, virtual technology was not merely emerging but already almost dominant. In those same years, however, they interpreted what was taking shape as an anthropological phenomenon more perilous than television, which was then a centre of the power of political and psychological influence. They were travelling on parallel paths, one taking a more Wittgensteinian approach, the other a sort of hermeneutic one.

Aiming to defend the values of rationality and modernity, Tomás Maldonado (1922–2018), studied the relations between technology and culture and, in the early 1990s, examined the central issue of the evolution of the current epoch of human civilization, the Anthropocene, as it is called today – namely, the crucial issue of the real and the virtual. In this context, where the most interesting and most disturbing aspects of technological simulation emerge, Maldonado attempts to rethink the concept of reality and its representations (1992). In his telling, it was precisely in 1930 when the illusory universe of virtual reality came to the fore, a universe in which the operator-visitor-observer seemed to become the agent in processes that exploit artificial elements and make them behave as though they were real. Maldonado assesses the risks and promises of this epochal challenge with a careful analysis of visual representations in their historical development, highlighting in the process factors of great symbolic and social importance, from iconoclasm to "iconophilia," from Renaissance perspective to photography, cinema, television, computer graphics, and robotics.

In his 1992 book *Reale e virtuale*, the author focuses on visual materials and their dematerialization while identifying a new "concreteness" created by operational and communicative aspects of virtuality not reducible to an idea of images as intangible and illusory, or ghostly and phantasmic. In fact, software is a technology, a cognitive tool that contributes both directly and indirectly to material changes in "thought technologies." After the long transition from orality to writing, another momentous transition obtained, the printed word, with the age of the printing press, which marks the start of modernity, to the high-definition images of today. Like other techniques of artistic-literary representation, perspective was produced in conjunction with the system of optics developed in the fifteenth century by Filippo Brunelleschi, Leon Battista Alberti, Piero della Francesca, and Leonardo da Vinci, who all followed in the footsteps of Arab mathematician Alhazen (d. 1039). Yet we need to think of perspective together with ceroplastics and the realist-naturalist artistry in other historical periods, and then we need to consider how the quest for the "real" evolves up to the creation of anthropomorphic robots. In the industrial society of the second half of the nineteenth century, this drive toward realism develops further into mass "mediatization," with realist novels, newspapers, and graphic illustrations. In the twentieth century, it becomes global visual spectacle, a democratization of entertainment that advertising, cinema, and later television, as ritualized spaces of the double mirror of reality, enacted up to the 1960s, culminating in a digital aesthetics toward the end of the last century. At this point an "empire of trompe l'oeil" obtains, rejuvenated by technologies that eliminate the oneiric and private sphere, replacing it with the pretense of a different reality, a more real and authentic one. As Maldonado states, this regime of visuality amounts to

> a trompe l'oeil that, unlike in the past, resurfaces armed with a formidable capacity for propagation on a mass scale. It is everywhere and accessible to everyone … Ours has definitely been a civilization of images. We can accept this definition even if, on closer inspection, all civilizations have been civilizations of images. This definition would be truer if we added that ours is a civilization in which a particular kind of images (owing to the contribution of new technologies of production and distribution of icons), or trompe l'oeil images, achieve a prodigious realistic effect especially if we consider the latest developments in the pursuit of virtual realities. (48; translated by Corrado Federici)

Following this visual revolution based on so-called digital models, we undoubtedly witness the emergence of unimaginable advances in computer modelling, design, and description; advances that unleash intellectual, cognitive, and sensory capabilities. In comparison with what was done for millennia in the realm of copying and giving form to objects, we now realize that we are no longer protagonists but objects of the modelling activity. Art, technology, and science proceed together, in an interlacement that is often not clearly distinguishable due to the nature of "doing" that has become detached from the naturalness of doing. When we create something, we immerse ourselves in the act of inventing, discovering, and innovating in a domain that appears to be shared by artists and scientists alike. But this is not the case, especially if we think of the workings of the human mind compared to those of the computer control device that moves a robotic limb, or of the connection between the human eye and an artificial one. Faced with the simulacrum of communication rather than the real thing, or the banalization of symbols reduced to the stereotypes of an endless playful recycling, we need to understand more clearly the object and its copy.

3 CONCERNING THE GOLDEN THREAD OF TRADITIONS

Elémire Zolla (1926–2002) devised an original interpretation of myth and symbol and thereby made an important contribution to comparative cultural studies in the process. He applied his knowledge of esoteric doctrines, as well as Eastern and Western mysticism, to a discussion of human beginnings and the Jungian archetypes that pertain to a spiritual journey that guides the flow of historical time. In 1959, with *Eclissi dell'intellettuale* (The eclipse of the intellectual), and then around May '68, he rejected not only the tastes of the political and cultural elite but also Marxist and semiotic interpretations of mass society and art. In doing so, he proposed different ways of thinking. His travels to various countries, from the United States to India, Indonesia, China, Korea, Myanmar (Burma), and Greece, inspired a variety of reflections that we find scattered throughout his books. Over the years, but especially in the 1970s, he commented on and edited the essays of Pavel Florensky, collected in *La Colonna e il fondamento della verità* (The pillar and the ground of truth) and *Le porte regali. Saggio sull'icona* (Royal doors: An essay on the icon). From the standpoint of historical and hermeneutic criticism, these writings provide important insights into Russian religious and philosophical culture. They depict neglected aspects of history, namely, visual culture, artistic legacy, and the contemplative safekeeping of being.

With regard to tradition, transcendentalism, and metaphysics, topics to which Zolla has made many contributions, I concentrate my attention here on two works: *Uscite dal mondo* (Ways out of the world, 1992) and *Che cos'è la tradizione?* (What is tradition?, [1971] 1998). Regarding the first book, we could say that twenty-five years ago the author erred regarding the new visual technologies. It is surprising that there he interprets virtual reality, at the time emergent but rapidly spreading, as a wholesome overturning of the Industrial Revolution "that turns everything upside down and puts it all in play again." On the contrary, what is especially evident today is virtual reality's imprisonment, not liberation, of the mind; there is no catharsis, no detachment from our passions. The future that was then at our doorstep. Virtual technologies, including holography (with the 3D glasses and a variety of laser devices), were supposed to activate sensors in the brain capable of transmitting the inner world of the individual to the external world and vice versa. With the aid of VR headsets and gloves, we were supposed to discover new realities – fly, detach ourselves from the terrestrial plane, or even glide over water and thus realize an ancient dream. Zolla was describing a human being who experiences freedom thanks to not only the feeling of ecstatic abandon but also the development of correlations between brain and computer for the purpose of enhancing the performance of human faculties. Making ourselves invisible, passing through solid objects in a burst of light, which might be deemed almost shamanic, and discovering an altered state of consciousness in the domain of light, were all supposed to bring to the fore a more authentic spiritual world that exists alongside and within the quotidian one. Special effects were supposed to produce a continuous flow of being, not unlike that allegedly produced by Buddhist meditation and syncretistic or Christian-ecstatic contemplative practice. All this within the framework of various ways of escaping the world, gleaned from the ancient past to the future, the archaic to the technological, where everyone would be immersed as initiates into the flow of a wondrous nature, outside of the ordinary coordinates of time and space in an unending healing process.

As far as Zolla was concerned, a life of heightened perception, emotion, and mental acuity, achieved without the use of hallu-cinogens, was emerging in all its unprecedented richness, even though the marketplace was always waiting in ambush and Zolla suspected that it would soon contaminate this surge of incredible expectations. Just as shamanic rituals in preliterate societies realized atavistic aspirations to communicate with the spirits of animals through various forms of artistic and ritual expression, modern shamanic-like rituals would be activated in the virtual world through a continuous transference of meaning and artistic depiction whose purpose was to make present, in an idealized form of participation made possible by technology, the continuum of human existence and that of all living organisms. We would find ourselves in a perfect state such as that described in ancient Hindu literature, where there is no desire, no anticipation of the future, no ties with the present, no memory of the past; where we are awake while sleeping and asleep while awake. Yet it could be argued that this is an illusion: computers, iPhones, and aug-mented reality are not the dawn of a new mode of perceiving and experiencing life.

At this point, two quotes are relevant to our discussion of the new sensibility, or the aesthetics of silence and slowness joined together with the myth of the aura. The first is an excerpt from the new edition of *Che cos'è la tradizione?*: "Tradition is made concrete through a series of expedients: sacraments, symbols, myths, rituals, and common definitions whose aim is to develop that part, faculty, or disposition of human beings that come into contact with the highest degree of being allowed, placing at the summit of their corporeal or psychological constitution spirit and intellectual intuition" (Zolla [1971] 1998, 121; translated by Corrado Federici).

Tradition is the transmission of the idea of being in its perfect form. In essence, transmission is a theophany. In other words, we are enmeshed in the beauty of nature, in its expansive wonder, or as the Greeks knew with respect to knowledge of the sensible world, a profane mysticism.

The second passage concerns the present human condition of disorientation on account of everything seemingly falling to pieces without explanation, in spite of advanced technology: "Common in dreams is the anguish of having an object nearby and not being able to reach out and grab it or having to utter a decisive word only to realize that it does not emerge from the throat. Modern human beings are such dreamers unable to attain the thing needed. They cannot utter the liberating word and do not know what prevents them from doing so" (Zolla [1971] 1998, 95).

Zolla goes on to claim that today there is disdain for contemplation that is reflected in academic studies, a disdain that produces everywhere much misunderstanding of what it means to be human. The need to reassert the right to contemplate appears to bring to mind, on the one hand, John Ruskin (the criteria for the depiction of nature in landscape painting, in *Modern Painters*) and, on the other hand, Rosario Assunto (the concept of active contemplation, in *Il paesaggio e l'estetica* [The landscape and aesthetics]).

Zolla therefore foresees a resurgence of contemplation (118–31). Quoting Aristotle, he claims:

But such a life would be too high for man; for it is not
in so far as he is man that he will live so, but in so far as
something divine is present in him; and by so much as this
is superior to our composite nature is its activity superior
to that which is the exercise of the other kind of virtue.
If reason is divine, then, in comparison with man, the life
according to it is divine in comparison with human life.
But we must not follow those who advise us, being men,
to think of human things, and, being mortal, of mortal

things, but must, so far as we can, make ourselves immortal, and strain every nerve to live in accordance with the best thing in us; for even if it be small in bulk, much more does it in power and worth surpass everything ... Quiet, contemplation, joy, and sky are linked together is a single node in the system of sacred intuitions present in our languages. (*Nicomachean Ethics*, 1177b)

Most important, contemplation is movement through which we free ourselves from preoccupation with contingent circumstances, passions, and interests individual and collective. When we contemplate, we stop saying "I" or "we" and we enjoy a perfect identification of inner and outer self. Contemplation is a way out, but it remains "a feeble dream" (Zolla [1971] 1998, 127) in everyday thinking.

4 WORLDVIEWS

The ideas connecting the readings from Maldonado and Zolla, from which others liberally drew, originated in a study of worldviews by Karl Jaspers in the 1920s: *Psicologia delle visioni del mondo* (The psychology of worldviews, 1950). There, we find an interpretation and conception of contemplation that are consistent with my approach to the theme of representation. Worldviews are forms of intuitive representation, ideas, manifestations, and expressions, all from the point of view of the subject and of the object in that we are dealing with two worlds melded together into a concrete form. The psychology of worldviews has four features or elements that are part of a system of mediation between the subject and the world: i) authenticity that emerges from the very essence of humanity to form a view that is not superficial or merely virtual, or based on reproduced images; ii) formalization that takes place between form and matter, between the indistinctness of form and the infinity of the idea; iii) differentiation or multiplicity as a vital aspect of the worldview, and, therefore, not a single worldview; and iv) absoluteness that nonetheless never resolves itself into a perfectly objective view, since it is the expression of life and energy that affirms itself in the multiplicity of forms activated by the description of intuited visions and representations of experiences connecting subject and object. Jaspers states:

> The image of the world in the active attitude can be seen in its effects and, I would like to say, in the coexistential sphere. The image of the world in the contemplative attitude, instead, is always in front of us, independent and untameable. We can only see and observe it; it is foreign to us. To know the world for the contemplative attitude means placing it in front of them; for the active attitude it means creating, making, and transforming it through its own actions. In the active attitude, the world must be reshaped to the point where the active can understand it as its own world. (66; translated by Corrado Federici)

There is a constant duality at play in activity where desire meets resistance. In contemplation, however, there is no domination; the spirit of possessing something is replaced by the desire to observe, to gaze upon the thing: the object is at a distance and one approaches it in order to immerse oneself in it. Here, we do not have merely sensory vision, or pure perception, because there is also a process of form making. The contemplative attitude is aesthetic in that it is a subjective attitude. Art and knowledge can spring from this even if, according to Jaspers, contemplation per se is neither art nor knowledge. "Self-reflectiveness implies that we see ourselves. The self that each of us sees does not exist, however, as a solid being. Rather, we catch glimpses of individual phenomena of our experience, individual connections, and we attribute these scattered fragments to an image of the self, as a whole entity" (Jaspers 1950, 108).

We confuse these fragments with the true, real self, which is never fully our object. Our self-knowledge is an infinite task that becomes clear only in vivid and emotional experience. These observations relate to the following specific analysis:

> Attitudes and images of the world are abstractions that separate what coexists in practice, that treat as an independent

> phenomenon what exists only in the service of, or as
> a phenomenon of, certain forces. Our understanding of
> worldviews deepens if we consider the problem of such
> forces, for which, and by virtue of which, those elements
> reconstitute themselves in their entirety … Those forces
> represent in the life of the mind as such the totalities
> from which, and only from which, elements are artificially
> extracted as words which in themselves do not have an
> independent existence. (Jaspers 1950, 255)

There is a relationship between the active attitude and the contemplative attitude; there is no opposition between them but rather a common articulation, with the latter promoting a seeing and a giving form for itself, a giving form that distances itself from the pretense of being captured by a single definition. In the face of the image of the historical-material world, as well as that of worlds spatial-temporal, psychological-cultural, mythic-demonic, and metaphysical, the contemplative attitude thrives on an aesthetic element, a state of isolation on account of which, as Immanuel Kant notes, we speak of "disinterested pleasure" or, for Arthur Schopenhauer, "negation of the will." The time for seeing, observing, and contemplating necessitates the founding of the ecstatic moment that always nourishes creativity and representation. The crucial factor in the aesthetic attitude is solitude; it frees itself from both the contents and the experience of determinant psychological relations, such as tasks, purposes, and dictates of the will. The aesthetic attitude of contemplation, however, does not mean experiencing captivation in order to avoid existence but rather experiencing a cathartic release (in the process of representation) in the face of the ephemerality of human existence. This is the core of what we call "spirit." Jaspers applies Kant's position, in which he wonders what is meant by "spirit," to language, poetry, painting, and sculpture. Jaspers interprets and comments as follows:

> In terms of aesthetics, spirit is the vivifying element of
> the soul … Now I claim that this principle is nothing other
> than the faculty of representing aesthetic ideas; by aesthetic

ideas I mean the representation of the creative imagination that stimulates us to think a great deal without, however, there being a specific thought or concept that corresponds adequately to the idea, and that, as a consequence, no language can fully capture or render wholly comprehensible. It is easy to see that it is the correlative, the pendant, of a notion of reason, which, conversely, is a concept to which no view or mental image can adequately correspond. Such mental images can be called ideas, on the one hand, because they tend to go beyond experience, and, on the other hand, no concept can adequately correspond to these internal views. (561–2)

Now for a general observation: seeing and representing from the point of view of those who create and those who enjoy what is created proceeds differently from the points of view of receiving subject and producing subject. Studies on the workings of the sensory system conclude that in both cases we find movement as well as the activity of the imagination because everyone has the capacity to perceive and to represent both externally and internally. Language and aesthetic-social value establish the differences between ordinary configurations and configurations that we call artistic; perceptions and representations are raw materials that are worked into forms onto which the motor activity of the eye intervenes as determined by the distance of the object relative to it. In essence, we find ourselves in the presence of an interaction among perceptual forms and actual forms, as described by Adolf von Hildebrand in his search for a criterion of pure visibility (*The Problem of Form in Painting and Sculpture*, 1893).

Actual forms do not exist except as the result of a natural movement of the eye and of a readjustment of sight that converts the object into a visual impression: the artistic effect transforms the perceptual aspect into a concrete image, which especially concerns architecture and sculpture as plastic arts. This is, as well, something that painters in ancient Greece already achieved in the form of imitative art and scenery painting. The real impressions of objects that are present to us coexist with the impressions of the representations of those same objects that we receive from the world of art.

5 THE AGONY OF CONTEMPLATION

The fact that contemplation has declined in importance or become outmoded nowadays stems from the new modes of copying, representing, producing, and reading images in line with the interpretative schemas examined to this point. Environments, architectural projects, and 3D paintings appear as immersive art featuring touchscreens (without keyboards or headsets) that create a virtual reality experience. This is the current fate of landscapes in a continuous perceptual and mental transformation. We are living in the digital and post-digital-holographic age that leads to the formulation of a new universal alphabet. What we call virtual reality is a simulated reality in which the observer, spectator, or even operator, intervenes interactively using an optical-tactile-auditory prosthetic device in a 3D environment generated by a computer connected to a laser. It is an artificial reality where space and the environment are virtual 3D images. Users of the apparatus inhabit a 3D space generated by the system, but they can also see it from the outside. Computer graphics embarked on this venture a few decades ago, programming images by applying an interactive principle with variable settings, forms, and colours. The simulated objects can be moved around an observer or they can be fixed while the observer moves, thereby producing a gallery of illusory images. With respect to this last point (the illusion aspect), Ernst Gombrich (1965, 278) observes that the pursuit of absolute realism in images simultaneously, and paradoxically, reinforces and weakens our relationship with the real. In fact, as we realize all too well today, the attainment of so-called perfect illusion also marked the onset of disillusionment because we can no longer distinguish illusion from reality and thus perfect illusion cannot be imagined. In essence, we must avoid equating progress in the naturalistic representation of space with presumed progress in art. To think otherwise would mean hypostasizing realism as if it were the only legitimate purpose of artistic creation. The evolution of visual technology does not mirror the evolution of art.

That said, I feel compelled to make a much-needed critique of the technical impact of illusory reproductions of the visible world produced on real or virtual platforms. Our world is by now almost completely virtualized. The fact that a real museum, for example, can be replaced by a virtual museum opens up a disconcerting scenario. We lose the authenticity of aesthetic-linguistic perception by accepting virtual depictions as real. The fact that, by wearing VR glasses and an *intelligent* glove or an *intelligent* suit, we are able to enter an illusory reality in order to *experience it* as though it were real, is tangible and practicable on a daily basis. We are constantly confronted with a body double; the copy replaces the original. It is as though we were inside a video game. A vicarious action is performed by our stand-in, our digital alter ego, in the sensible, imaginary world. Amid heated debate on reality and simulation, media theorist Norbert Bolz in the early 1990s reacted strongly to various criticisms regarding the digital aesthetics of simulation. What can we say today when, by means of mobile holograms, virtual reality is on the verge of assuming incommensurable proportions? Are we afraid of the death of reality? There is, of course, a great concern for the loss of the human dimension of knowing and feeling. Appearance does not correspond adequately to reality. The veil has been removed from the "new naturalness" that is completely technological and virtual.

Immersive art or the pleasure of visual-tactile immersion is a product of the history of visual technologies, from the plaster cast and stereoscope to the panorama and 3D cinema. It is an apparatus, a contrivance, and a diversion that nonetheless eliminates the system of nature and empathy, replacing it with a system that transforms the environment in a playful or artificially participatory way as it blunts the aesthetic-cognitive element and the agency of the subject. Touchscreens risk seriously falsifying reality: subjects find themselves in the condition of prisoners, unable to be protagonists in the mise en scène of the world. The environments created by simulation replace real ones while the activities of experiencing and imagining dissolve. The experience and awareness of simulation as well as processes involving artistic imitation, like those engendered by ancient Greek painters Zeuxis of Heraclea (b. 464 BCE) and Parrhasius of Ephesus (b. before 399 BCE), are one thing; substitution of the real thing is another. This, too, is certainly an aesthetic experience. We can convince ourselves that the touchscreen enables us to escape real space and makes it possible to achieve authentic freedom and "purification" from the corporeality of our senses. Certainly, escaping physical space is a form of flying above reality, and in that moment we are masters of our world; in that moment destiny seems to unfold in its entirety before our eyes. It is like experiencing salvation and freedom together. This appears to be the realization of the passage in Friedrich Nietzsche's *Thus Spake Zarathustra*, on "the spirit of gravity," which reads, "He who one day teacheth man to fly will have shifted all landmarks; to him will all landmarks themselves fly into the air; the earth will christen anew" (pt. 3, no. 11). It seems to some that virtual reality makes this happen, but this is not so. Virtual reality is not a form of freedom. It is, rather, a trap as we find depicted in such films as Barry Levinson's *Disclosure* (1994), Steven Spielberg's *A.I. Artificial Intelligence* (2001), or, more recently, Spike Jonze's *Her* (2103) or James Ponsoldt's *The Circle* (2017), the last featuring a female protagonist who works for a multinational social media company. From myth to prison then.

6 MIMESIS AND RESEMBLANCE: A MYTHOPOETIC STUDY

Forms, figures, gestures, words, sounds, and colours are the defining qualia of works of art; they appear in aesthetic acts of reproduction that change objects into images, representations, and expressions. Of course, we imitate, copy, and transform according to the pleasures of creative taste, which define our perceptions of the world utilizing either mimesis or fantasy, or a combination of these.

I introduce mimesis or imitation here in an effort to understand what representing and expressing mean. According to Aristotle, "the instinct of imitation is implanted in man in childhood, one difference between him and other animals being that he is the most imitative of living creatures, and through imitation learns his earliest lessons" (*Poetics* 1448 b7). Historically, imitation has a wide range of meanings, from emulation to idealization of models, from realist mirroring to trompe l'oeil illusions. It has to do with the image and mimesis, and, therefore, with permanence and change across time.

Representation works through figures, signs, tangible symbols, and (in processes that are sometimes non-material) other objects or aspects of reality. In general, it refers primarily to images of all kinds, pictorial, graphic, sculptural, literary, rhetorical, theatrical, cinematic, televised, and virtual. At times, it can be symbolic, as when the dove represents peace. Described more fully, it comes in a range of technical and scientific formats, from cartography to icon design, from graphic to holographic reproduction, and from the illustration of multivariable functions to the geometric representation of real numbers. In this mass of illustrations and schemas, there is a vast interplay between reality and appearances, illusions, fictions, and symbols; this involves a mental process that starts with the senses and moves beyond imitation and reproduction, beyond description and illustration, in an unfolding of languages situated somewhere between naturalism (or realism) and the world of fantasy. By analogy, such a cluster of processes can be considered as an image in a dual sense, both as reproduction of what the senses perceive and mental image of a sensation, the latter to the point where it is an internal reflection of the object perceived. They concern both concrete objects and physical properties (energy, force) and abstract ideas (categories or numbers). We could say that image and representation are, per Jean-Paul Sartre and Edmund Husserl, inseparable terms. But representation does not remain contained within concepts: it frees itself in a gesture of aesthetic freedom capable of giving form to the invisible, unreflective, and indeterminate. Representation is the ensemble of processes through which emerge perceptions, images, and judgments that the mind exhibits to itself as a substitute for something, whether an object, person, event, or phenomenon.

Representing is, in essence, making the vastness of the real present, but in doing so it is not disconnected from expressing, which literally (as in *ex-press*) means pressing something out in order to obtain the nectar or essence. This is not a matter of making the domain of expression correspond to the interiority or subjectivity of the artist. We can, instead, see how the act of manifesting involved in the creation of graphic symbols corresponds to a world of impressions, impulses, emotions, and feelings shared by the artist and the viewer of the artwork. Furthermore, in the experience of art, the act of representing and expressing cannot avoid converging in one, and this occurs because the artist performs a number of so-called discrete actions at once—*movere* (to move), *docere* (to teach), and *delectare* (to please)—which are procedures that come into existence when the aesthetic act becomes an artistic act. In the artistic creation of forms and figures, even if they are abstract or presumably scientific, ambiguous or allusive elements prevail for the most part, thereby inducing an unrestricted flow of aesthetic taste among the domains of representation, expression, reception, and enjoyment. We could imagine this to be true, and equally to the same extent, in the archaic and modern periods, and in the contemporary age as well. The personal style of the artist, the subject of this analysis, functions in the same way in both the figurative and the non-figurative arts. There is a dialectic between the figurative and non-figurative elements of design throughout the history of artistic culture, which suggests clear parallels with wave spectrum representations of electromagnetic fields and illustrations of geometric fractals; this dialectic always occurs, however, within the framework of the ambiguity and polysemy of the acts of perceiving and representing that characterize aesthetic and artistic gestures. Despite its towering importance, Renaissance perspective is but one way of looking at nature. Art and science represent two distinct activities, even though, for example, Eric R. Kandel (2017) does not share this opinion and prefers to take a neuroscientific approach.

As early as 1954, Luigi Pareyson, in *Estetica. Teoria della formatività* (Aesthetics: A theory of formativity), noted the link between contemplation and interpretation, a link he underscores in the introduction to the 1988 edition of his book. He states that contemplation is the enjoyment of the beautiful as the end product of the act of interpretation: contemplation, in which image and thing converge, resulting in the attainment of knowledge. Since, in fact, interpretation is a process of formation, that is to say, a process of invention and production that culminates in a state of calmness or composed serenity in the viewer, interpretation is contemplation because in its dynamic unfolding it proffers images in which the work and the experience of figuration culminate. The process of interpretation then invents new structures as it gradually calibrates the degree of correspondence between the image and the thing along the various phases of production intended to create a form that encompasses and concludes the act of figuration itself. The calmness confirms the success of the invention, the finalization of the formation process; aesthetic attention, with all its tensions, subsides in silent and calm contemplation, a perfect correlation between the contemplating and the contemplated. In other words, we see form as form – but what does it mean to see form as form? It means having completed its interpretation, having uncovered its meaning and its secret; it means that the "the gaze has become insightful, and therefore contemplative" (Pareyson 1988, 195; translated by Corrado Federici). This process is necessarily accompanied by a pleasure that is part of the anxiety of the searching and waiting that drive it, as well as of the pausing in a sort of complete contentment in the end. Interpreting, then, implies representing and being absorbed in the image. For these reasons "the gaze of one who contemplates enjoys the view of the form as such, and the view of the form, with its harmony and internal perfection, satisfies the gaze as it scans the form's parts while it circles ideally through the very coherence that binds it in a defined and perfect whole" (Pareyson, 195).

The form of finality (or mode of representing), as well as the expression of harmony and perfection in conformity with the norms of coherence and balance between the parts and the whole, creates the beauty, though untouched by extrinsic references and removed from both objectivity and subjectivity, that reveals form as form. In aesthetic pleasure, as it relates to both artistic beauty and natural beauty, contemplation entails surprise and promotes a state of wonder. What stirs us emotionally combines with the momentary pause that stops all motion; aesthetic contemplation generates a motionless pleasure, while surprise is accompanied by a certain movement, which can potentially distract. As regards natural beauty, its contemplation presupposes the formative power of nature in the sense that it is itself the result of a formative process. In brief, we can say that in consideration of the foregoing production, contemplatability, formation, and contemplation are inseparably linked. The possibility of contemplation itself as the completion of a process of interpretation is bound up with other presuppositions in a philosophy of personhood where connections between formativity, hermeneutics, and beauty come together as one.

Gillo Dorfles also considers the question of the image and the imagination in particular, and he emphasizes the importance of the formative process as *Gestaltung* (design or composition), which implies not only the innate formativity present in all processes, both human and natural, but also the formativity of the imagination, that is to say, the activity of the human mind beyond the phenomenal toward which perception draws us. Some formal components of artworks possess a temporal dimension by virtue of which they appear very different from when first conceived and realized. In *Divenire delle arti* (*The becoming of the arts*, [1959] 1971), Dorfles provides an especially interesting point of consideration by way of "synesthesia" or interplay among the arts. Typical examples of synesthesia include colour images evoked by sounds, "sound images" evoked by colours, and chromatic images evoked by words. These images are produced by the sensory capacity of the subject and/or the associative structure of the object. It is a structure whose importance in aesthetics and art should not be underestimated, Dorfles argues:

What we must remember is not so much the search for similar examples in works by different authors as the task

of determining whether such interrelation or interaction
between sensory images and aesthetic images allows us
to hypothesize the existence of a constant rapport between
the elements of perception and the elements of creativity
(and reception) in the work of art … The sharpness of
some sensory stimuli relates directly to the human faculty
of imagination, so much so that we could hazard a guess
that precisely this exalted quality of the imagination is
one of the main reasons for the impulse to create and
to appreciate the work of art. (Dorfles, 480; translated
by Corrado Federici)

7 FROM THE CLASSIC TO THE BAROQUE

After these initial observations, we could say that representation
is the result of contemplation, that is to say, the act of looking
at an object near us and at the same time of being absorbed into
that object through the pleasure of losing ourselves and finding
out-of-the-ordinary meaning in the life we live. This is similar
to an ecstatic experience in some ways, a going out of ourselves
and into a state of intense feelings.

We can understand the meaning of representation in relation
to sensibility through two examples separated in time: Piero
della Francesca's *La città ideale* (The ideal city, circa 1470) and
the mannerist sculptures in the sixteenth-century Gardens of
Bomarzo, located northwest of Rome. We could perhaps say
that aesthetics has always been understood, and not only in the
West, in relation to two faculties: that of creating representations
and that of sensory perception, which intersect, blend together,
or remain distinct throughout not only the history of the visual
and plastic arts but also the evolution of our feeling for nature.
In *La città ideale*, located in the Ducal Palace in Urbino, the
dominant feature is its play on perspective. Its beauty rests on
proportion, balance, symmetry, and composed serenity: the space
is homogeneous, rational, abstract, and infinite, produced by an
artist who draws his inspiration from classical and ideal forms.
In Bomarzo, on the other hand, we *directly* experience emotions
associated with tactility. In the mannerist and baroque forms,

the contact of skin with man-made products is enhanced by the prevailing sense of a unity of a participatory perception, which tends to surprise and delight visitors who are eager to encounter the monstrous (the Gardens is also called the Park of the Monsters). Here beauty is the product of sensations. To illustrate this second faculty (of sensory perception), we could, taking our cue from Andrea Pinotti, refer to the masters of empathy, nineteenth- and twentieth-century German philosophers Robert and Friedrich T. Vischer, Theodor Lipps, Johannes Volkelt, and Moritz Geiger, for whom the human subject is a psychosomatic unity, an amalgam of body and soul (Pinotti 1997). We could also mention the masters of the theory of form, such as psychologist and phenomenologist Wolfgang Köhler, or the proponents of the "aesthetics of atmosphere," who worked in the wake of Herman Schmitz and Gernot Böhme, as Tonino Griffero (2010) suggests.

The climate of recent years compels me to criticize the new technical virtuality, against which also converge the qualities that in the distant past, from India and China to the West, were directed at recovering the values of contemplation. Held hostage by the clash of different interpretations of truth originating in the "new realism" and hermeneutics, especially concerning the symbolic models of *noeta* (objects of thought) and *aistheta* (perceptible things), knowledge today distinguishes mental images from signs. The stereotypes of seeing and knowing come to light passing through naturalism and ontologism, or the relation between matter and intentionality. On the basis of these reflections, we can essentially see how the internet appears to obstruct or disturb the contemplative state, the internal organization of one's relationship with the object. It is difficult to humanize digital technology. The web is an apparatus designed for entertainment, information, and communication; it is rare to find an ethics of artificial intelligence and virtual reality, at least in these times and with these products. Artificial intelligence disregards human mediation, despite the fact that the seductive strategies of graphic design and media persuade us that the opposite is true.

Aesthetic-artistic practices that restore techniques of silence, slowness, and harmonious forms, i.e., expressions that rethink our relationship with nature and the landscape, such as environmental art, earth art, green architecture, and new forms of gardening in the context of urban art, are possible manifestations of the distant echo of Virgil's *Eclogues*. It is one of the earliest texts to provide a representation of natural space as an environment that is both internal and familiar, the product of a poetics of place and a humanization of the natural world, processes created through complex, long-term transformations in the term *physis* or nature, which, only a short time earlier, in Lucretius, had a physical or corporeal meaning. It was not, therefore, the flamboyant "nature" of technologies, rock concerts held in inappropriate places, or the noises of city party-goers that held the meaning of silence hostage. Rather, in the face of the beauty of ancient towns and neighbourhoods devastated by graffiti artists and the most vulgar expressions of street painting that transform perception and sight into a labyrinth of the kind we might find in a comic book nightmare, in the face of the sheer consumerist aspect of the impoverishment of fantasy, deprived of myth, metaphor, and the value of dreams, the need arises to search for an aesthetic taste that is hidden and solitary but slowly re-emerging. For an entire century, a distorted newness, caused by the banal and the shocking in the field of art, has finally merged with virtual and digital techniques that steal meaning away from the profundity of emotions and relationships. Works of art on our cellphones, augmented reality, and VR glasses are recent illusions that disperse the receptive and creative gaze, mesmerizing it without engaging it, and subduing it as it makes spontaneous naturalness vanish.

8 ON THE NATURE OF REPRESENTATION

I now return to the original topic of representation for additional remarks. I often wonder whether aesthetics can be considered a philosophy of representation since it directs attention to the dual reality of mental objects, separating the contemplative gaze from the life of *aesthesis*. For this reason, I am attempting to shed light on the abstract or neutral aspect of beauty, without excluding the living component of things and feelings. In experiencing art we also note the creativity of aesthetic reception, when in our times we interpret the "death of art" as not an end but an opening up to a multiplicity of evocative, perceptual, and formative elements. Faced with so many works by so many authors, as well as non-narrative films, works of environmental and land art, minimalist music, ambient music, and deconstructive architecture, I wonder, along with Federico Vercellone (2013), what remains of art apart from beauty, and what remains of beauty apart from the art? Perhaps only an image? On the other hand, with these epochal transformations, the body, as Jean-Luc Nancy (2014) contends, has been transformed: it is no longer a container for thought or being. It has liquefied; it has become attitude or posture. There is an unease with, or enthusiasm for, change, depending on the point of view we want to consider.

We could overcome this condition by choosing and observing art and aesthetics and by withdrawing from what have now become a habitual recourse to shock, novelty, provocation, ephemeralness, as well as by rediscovering contemplation, the source of aesthetics and art. When we embrace a philosophy that is sensitive to these matters, and we take note of the need for a hermeneutics of the image, we situate ourselves comfortably in the company of Hans-Georg Gadamer, Richard Rorty, and Arthur Danto and their studies on these matters.

The term *representation* can be interpreted in either subjective or objective terms. In subjective terms, it refers to the mind's presenting of something to itself, whether an external object or a mental state, as an object that belongs to it; in objective terms, representation is the object itself as represented, that is to say, a fact that is present in consciousness. Both the act of presenting and the fact of representation – the former, more so – can be studied from a philosophical and a psychological point of view. We should take into account both the mind's capacity for placing an object before itself and the way this activity or mechanism of mental functioning unfolds quite apart from the study of the relationships between subject and object and the nature of the object. The first aspect of the relationship between subject and object is essentially gnoseological, or, rather, it concerns the very essence of the problem of knowledge insofar as it concerns the possibility and modes of this knowledge. Because when dealing with the conscious mind, which necessarily implies the knower and the known, we cannot avoid analyzing the nature of the latter in relation to the former. The study of representation, according to Fernando Gil, cannot but overlap with the field of metaphysics. The three possible solutions to the "metaphysical" problem that has cropped up entail three different formulations of the epistemological problem. First, the skeptical solution states that the nature of the represented object is unknowable and its very existence problematic, due to the absolute absence of a guaranteed correspondence between representation and object, thereby negating the epistemological problem or, better, declaring it unsolvable. Second, the realist solution posits the existence of the object independent of any activity on the part of the subject, focusing on the relations between the subject and the object and giving rise to solutions that range from naïve faith in the absolute fidelity of the representation in relation to the real object to a sort of epistemological skepticism that declares the representation of the object as such impossible and resolves itself into phenomenalism. Third, the idealist solution rejects all distinctions between subject and object, between being and thought, and considers the latter to be the cause of the former, rather than posing the epistemological problem in a different manner (which seems to confuse the problem with metaphysics, and, inasmuch as it makes the represented object a product of the representor, the idealist solution also eliminates the distinction between the subjective and the objective meaning of the term *representation*).

9 EXERCISES IN EKPHRASIS

The ancients were familiar with the term *representation*. Plato considered it to be a mirror image of sensible objects (*Republic*), and he also distinguished true images from false ones on the basis of whether or not they resembled the object reproduced (*Sophist*), that is to say, whether they constitute representations or products of the imagination. Aristotle, and later Thomas Aquinas, continued to probe this issue with extraordinary sensitivity. In modern philosophy the meaning of representation undergoes a profound change: its centre of gravity shifts from the object to the subject. But let us not lose sight of the ancient thinkers. For example, on the educational value of "typical" images, Plato still has something to teach us. His most recent interpreters include Jean-Jacques Wunenburger (1999; 2013), who argues that the Greek philosopher acknowledged that under certain circumstances images could lead to truth. In fact, he identifies in Plato the presence of a *typos* or pattern that permits us to rediscover the unseen connection between copy and original. In the plastic arts, the *typos* is a template or an imprint: in the metaphoric, pedagogical context, it is an imprint left by Ideas on the human soul, an imprint that guarantees a kind of fidelity between original and copy. Some passages in the *Dialogues* in fact seem to concede the existence of a dynamic bond between the image and essence. The perceptual experience of some images, especially artistic ones, reawakens in us an innate sense capable of leading us from the image back to its reason for existing. In other words, in perceptual experience, the objective dissimilarity of the image, whether in the case of mythological narrative or plastic representation, is not incompatible with an anagogic transformation that permits it to return to the essential source of what is represented without being captivated by idols or false notions.

Stated differently, the illusory structure of the image in allegory (for instance, in the *Republic*'s myth of the cave) is displaced by a self-referential search for the original, in that every soul is potentially open to the truth that lies dormant within it. Platonic "typicality," starting with the release of the prisoner in the cave, initiates an alternative practice, claims Wunenburger, one less iconoclastic than the discourse on principles. This practice permits some souls to pass through images in order to access their essence without losing themselves in seeming illusions that are "harmful to the mind." In this sense a "beautiful education," or education in the ways of the beautiful, can be a preparatory phase in certain arts, music, and poetry, which constitute the stages of an ascent that allows one to go from the idol back to the icon and from the icon to true essence. We could perhaps say, as does Wunenburger, that there exist two poles in Plato's teaching: on the one hand, pure form, intuitive knowledge (with no language, no image of essences), which is more implied than described; and on the other hand, impure form, tied to artistic practices, invented schemas, and deceptive words in a city inhabited by sophists and poets. This is a situation that in some ways we also find today in the society of simulation, spectacle, and technical reproduction, with its display of mass media projected images. But between the poles there is a whole intermediate world, which is the aesthetic (and artistic) one in which we live. Thus, we discover that we experience a hybrid, uncertain, and ambivalent ekphrasis where fictions abound. On the one hand, fictive contents touch the souls and make them feel that they are in direct contact with things, with visual images restored to their *typoi*; on the other hand, they tend to return to a philosophical ideal that strives for ultimate knowledge of essential truth. We pass from the visibility of the invisible that eludes the domination of the *eidola* (idealized figures or objects) to a continuous simulation and illusion of the original. We dwell in a place of crossings, where we find intersecting languages and visual representations. Perhaps this is a non-place of truth but a necessary and happy one, namely, art.

From these arguments based on a philosophy of representation, the image cannot be only a form of mirroring. It is also a possible opening up of itself to contemplation from the perspective of today's art. In this way we would valorize the broad range of descriptions of ekphrasis that has produced a genealogy of splendid analogies from antiquity to the Renaissance and indeed almost up to the present time.

I start with this general observation in order to enter into the details of the present analysis: one could say that a living being participates in the infinite, and each of us has something of the infinite within us. We cannot fully understand the existence of living beings in their quest for perfection, even of the most limited kind, except by framing life essentially within the immense entirety of matter in which we all coexist. We perceive, make concretely our own, and imagine what is common to all human beings. But to what forms of representation does our mind respond? The artistic, scientific, and technical world operates on a level similar, or apparently similar, to that of the ordinary aesthetic life, and the concept of "formative energy" plays an important role in that life. From the unleashing of that energy comes the impression that the entirety of nature cannot be compressed into the act of observing a single object within the whole. We might also suspect that the cognitive clarity of rationality and the representation of its expanding capabilities, as well as the most precise mirroring performed by the external senses, are inadequate. All existing relations in that immense dimly intuited totality set in motion by formative energy must necessarily become visible, audible, or otherwise perceptible by the imagination. Throughout the course of history, the infinite has been studied in biology and philosophy, the natural sciences, and aesthetics. But how can we represent the individual object within the whole? How can we imagine the totality of living things? How can we relate such an image to representation, the imagination to the collective imaginary? We find answers to these questions in the premises of a theory of form and formation.

10 INCARNATIONS OF UNREFLECTIVE CONSCIOUSNESS

Jean-Paul Sartre (1936, 1938, 2007) attempts to solve a complex set of problems related to the theme of the present book by using a phenomenological approach. The issue has been with us from antiquity, but it is in seventeenth-century philosophy all the way through to psychology in the first decades of the twentieth century that the problem has become increasingly compounded. Put simply, the question revolves around the relationship between *eikasia* (the initial mental image of the object) and *phantasia* (appearance), as well as around the complex mental processes implicit in representing and imagining. Sartre acknowledged there is a great deal of ambiguity on this topic, an ambiguity that spawns an entire discussion on vision-appearance, perception, intellect, memory, consciousness, and freedom, as well as ideas on sense and reason, representability and thinkability, meaning and phenomenon, subject and object. Thus, we find ourselves in the domain of an ontology of the image where, as within a single composite setting, the panoramas of aesthetics and epistemology are illuminated. Examining my own arguments in the light of Sartre's, I must concede, in spite of everything, the importance of this approach, especially nowadays when the evolution of technology tends to make us lose our sense of reality and revel in the imaginary world of simulation. In Sartre's analysis the Husserlian principle of intentionality is set against the doctrine of associationism and the experimentalism of Alexander Bain, Wilhelm Wundt, and Théodule Ribot; and representation is seen as involving an autonomous act that can give meaning to originary sensory data. For Sartre, the imagination is consciousness and, as such, it cannot be considered a merely reproductive faculty. In the conscious mind, we do not witness a spectacle of objects that appears outside of it but rather an intentionality of consciousness directed toward the real object in a process of "de-realization." Unlike the real object, which is subject to sensation and perception, the mental image is (creatively) free. The imagination exists in the aura of unreflective consciousness. In fact, we recognize that there is a level of existence that pertains to things, a level of presence, and another level that pertains to images, a level of absence. There is a simple reference dynamic at play whereby simulacra and idols exist in themselves, like the objects that correspond to them. Sartre contends that psychologists for the most part are confused by the "doctrine of the image" formulated by René Descartes, Baruch Spinoza, Gottfried Wilhelm Leibniz, David Hume, and Henri Bergson. The theory of the image is postulated outside of the theory of knowledge; psychologists confuse identity of essence with identity of existence. Only Husserl notes that perception and image are two intentional *Erlebnisse* (experiences of which one is cognizant) and that there is a distinction between *noesis* (concrete interior reality) and *noema* (meaning that inhabits that reality). Intentionality is a noetic act; it is at the root of the real world and the world of the imagination; it acts like an active synthesis in invented realities as well, whereas perception is passive synthesis. The analysis of consciousness is increasingly developed in Sartre's works from the second half of the 1930s. This is where we have, essentially, Sartre's engagement and his twin invitation to avoid reifying the image and place ourselves phenomenologically at a distance from illusions of immanence. The image is like "the incarnation of unreflective consciousness" (Sartre 2007, 226; translated by Corrado Federici). It does contain thought, but it is an intuitive one that emanates an aura of unreality. For this reason, our attitude before the image will be radically different from our attitude toward objects. The image has a magical quality, an enchantment that makes the object contemplated appear as the object desired in such a way that the mind can possess the object. For Sartre, mental objects are mere passivity, lack of definition, or empty mould; their fragility derives from our spontaneity. The essential structure of the image is the not-being-there of the entirely isolated object, which I can penetrate only by losing myself. I behave in the awareness of the unreality of the object. Sartre continues his description excluding or, at least, weakening the intervention of the will. For him, mental objects do not have a very long life and are rather independent of will. These objects have a discontinuous, jerky quality and do not provoke behaviours; they are quasi-sensible things that (in a transcendental move) incorporate, in a representational "mesh," knowledge of the world, not a list of objects. In these observations we can hear echoes of Kant's theory of the free play of the imagination but only initially, because the image, in Sartre's view, is an interior form of energy to which the human being is the witness. This is a nihilistic energy that in an aesthetic-creative perspective can turn into something positive. In the context of the imagination, we can return to the theme of the ambiguity of consciousness that is equally removed from being and its own being and, at the same time, from the concrete world. This very ambiguity of the act of knowing renders the aesthetic life vigorous in its countless, changing forms. In today's media society, the world of images, caught as it is between reality and virtuality, can no longer be understood as a world in which nothing happens in the Sartrean sense. Rather, it is a world in which nothing reveals itself, precisely on account of a ludic suspension of the existent: the society of the spectacle in the web of artificial intelligence.

We can now look at the image of nature as it relates to representation and the will from a different perspective, namely, Schopenhauer's. In our discussion of the image of the world and infiniteness, and the world and finiteness, what is interesting is the fact that prior to Schopenhauer, Johann Wolfgang von Goethe formulated the idea of a "formative impulse," and stressed that in inorganic nature nothing remains in its original state. Schopenhauer confronted the same problem of the truth of nature as he explored the theme of the identification of the body with the will. And this formative element is a key point in my reflections on the possibility of positing the entire world as a sculpture and living body, which is different from Sartre's position, which develops a dualistic view of the image. In *The Metaphysics of Nature* (Schopenhauer 2017), this body is given to the subject of the act of knowing in two different ways: as representation in the intuition of the intellect, an object among other objects governed by their laws; and as *will*, which is something of which we have immediate and complete knowledge. Each act of the will is immediately a movement of the body as well; the subject cannot really will the act without simultaneously perceiving that in representation the act looks like a movement of the body. The action of the body is the action of the objectified will, that is, the will has become an object that has become intuited. Will and representation constitute the entire essence of reality. Individuals are unable to represent their will clearly to themselves without the body, as emotions and inner world are implicated in this activity. This identity is by nature completely special, and it cannot be placed in one of the four semantic categories of logical, empirical, metaphysical, or metalogical truth. It is not a relation among abstract representations. It is the expression of a judgment relative to the interconnections among intuitive representation, the body, and what is not at all representation but something that is different from it *toto genere* (in all of its kind), i.e., the will. In the sense of will as illuminating knowledge, we have therefore come to understand the world itself as a living sculpture behind which we discover the "formative impulse" spoken about by Goethe.

11 ELEMENTS OF ACTIVE CONTEMPLATION

The beautiful has always seemed to be associated with a sort of unease. Today, attention tends to be directed to the truth of the work of art, which consists in the creative-formal act independent of content. Faced with the decline of the aura, which began with the advent of new media and twentieth-century avant-gardes, the reader is invited here to rediscover the roots of the most fervid origins of creative activity, i.e., *poiesis*, and possibly to go beyond the prevailing kitsch. In the present work, I interpret the contemplated image as *poietic* movement. According to some, the truth of the work of art today should consist in a concrete play of forms independent of ideas. Inspired by Hans Belting (2010), this is what Federico Vercellone (2013) believes as regards the rampant tendency to homologize, and he also identifies an anthropological need for form in which beauty regains full meaning in the world. But since canons of taste have disappeared and an unprecedented diversity in the reception and enjoyment of artworks has taken their place, how does the image function – in a process of resignification beyond object, copy, the blurring of contours, and indefiniteness of content? This is the open field of the present postmodern condition. The image is increasingly the release of symbolic energy, the surpassing of the conceptual, and the power of the gaze that incorporates both subject and object. Its nature is not simply duplicative but potentially revelatory. There are images endowed with a special and, let us say, projective impact that open up new possible worlds and images destined to be illusions. We can determine their impact, starting with their symbolic power and contemplate, per Vercellone, a "re-enchantment of the world" through a reformulation of a word that can restore tactile and universal images at the same time.

Belting advances the idea of a critical anthropology of the image, one that has as its object not only the primacy of the artistic act but also the analysis of the triad image, medium, and body. The medium is the physical material; the image, the event; and the body, the site where images are formed. However, in the long course of its technical evolution, the image exists in the practices of the new virtuality and its applications. Here, a current field is the mobile holographic image; in the present Anthropocene age, unimagined relations between living beings and things can be created. Expanded material forms will soon be confused with their mobile holographic reproductions. What is the value of experience in the face of a work of art reproduced in a mobile hologram? A desire for omnipotence is an attempt to dominate and enslave. This is the situation of the third millennium, and we need to understand the function of representation in the broadest sense of the term in order to provide possible explanations for the new mythologies.

12 TOWARD A WORLD OF FANTASY AND DREAM

Representation is tied to perception, memory, and social function. It is not simply reproduction but also, as has been noted, an active process that entails anticipation, learning, and cognitive development. It is a symbolic activity that involves invention, expression, and imitation.

Representation is multifaceted, as we see clearly in Edmund Husserl (*Cartesian Meditations*) and Ludwig Wittgenstein (*Tractatus*). Reflecting, imitating, and presenting, as well as making present, simulating, imprinting, expressing, and imagining, all revolve around some reflections on context: Representation takes the place of the represented, draws from itself its own representativeness, describes the represented, and itself constitutes a mirror image of the represented. The represented is represented by the representation, and, in turn, representation represents itself within a cognitive apparatus and is the creation of a subject. In essence, we understand that there is not merely one system of correspondences between the elements of a representation and the represented object, insofar as the object depends on the form of the figuration and on its own capacity to create relationships in thought, language, and communication. This can be established starting with Plato's *typos* and following the path of the educational function of "typical" images suggested by Wunenburger.

Let us, however, as a challenge, take the time to confront the concepts of proximity and distance as they relate to the object whose image we have before us and on which we pause to reflect. Let us try to think the object as object, and in the process preserve the essence of the object, ensuring that it is restored to the region where it resides. As Martin Heidegger explains, "Thinging is the nearing of world. Nearing is the nature of nearness. As we preserve the thing qua thing we inhabit nearness. The nearing of nearness is the true and sole dimension of the mirror-play of the world" (1976, 179).

This last sentence refers specifically to an image that the nearing of nearness creates or promotes: it is the authentic and sole dimension of the mirror-play of the world. The whole problem of the image and the thing, of the object and its double, in its variable and lively capacity to multiply, acquires concrete form that we feel within us, that mirror-play of the world. If there is no nearness, the thing vanishes and is wiped out. But when we distance ourselves from human agency and activity, we follow the backward motion of a thinking that represents, which is to say, toward a thinking that recollects. This process enables the creation of the correspondence, the mirror-play of the world, on account of which the thing is simple and malleable, not very "apparent." The thing is a thing in an active sense; language allows us to enter and dwell in it: "Whatever becomes a thing," says Heidegger, "occurs out of the mirror-play of the world" (179). In the measureless mass of men as living beings, something appears that is simple, unadorned, the thing as thing. And from here, from the thing that has come to light in images, emerges its relationship with the world. "Men alone, as mortals, by dwelling attain to the world as world. Only what conjoins itself out of world becomes a thing" (180). And it becomes, or will become, a thing thanks to the "mirror-play of the world": a swirl of image-things or thing-images.

Starting with distance and nearness, if we now observe, the images of the world in the context of the history of art, we are struck by what Maurice Merleau-Ponty called the "prose of the world" (1984). All human actions, like all words, are unfinished, caught in a spiral of inexhaustibility. The experience of expression relies on the fact that language generates images. We proceed from here, therefore, always keeping in mind the activities we have identified: perceiving, looking, representing, imagining, and feeling.

At this point, reasserting the value of the aesthetic and artistic realm, images appear to have a degree of truth, and, by virtue of this fact, a degree of really unusual ambiguity, which we can also interpret as a degree of efficacy. If we now examine and develop the metaphor of the mirror as well as the space of the fantastic, the thing takes another interesting turn. Roger Caillois saw in the fantastic something different from the surprising and unexpected element we find in fables and myths. For him, the identity and authenticity of the fantastic are created by the way the object is treated by the subject and by the disruption of conventions developed in the course of the history of the interpretation of the fantastic mode. In this analysis the fantastic possesses a hidden treasure that enchants us and a mystery that seduces us. This is because we can see in things a grand and captivating wonder that emerges amid indistinct signs and secrets, in depths and on surfaces. By comparison, the universe explored by Jurgis Baltrušaitis conveys, rather than an exaltation of the fantastic, the "wonders of the heart," that is to say, the liveliest and most thrilling part of our doing and imagining: an ensemble of extraordinary things. His interpretation, however, touches on, and at times fully treats, certain aspects of the fantastic that Caillois describes, especially where they both attempt to reach what is hidden or arcane, beyond the established forms and beyond the canons of connotative and historical classification. Baltrušaitis aspires not to describe a particular aesthetic knowledge or a particular form of creative intelligence, as much as to shed light on humanity's special memory, the legacy of markers and traces with their own identities that is often underappreciated and yet crucial. It is a memory produced by deciphering strange allegories, visual and emotional "dystonia," unusual iconological juxtapositions, unforeseen genealogies, and exciting hybrid delights. We can find a certain compatibility of views in Caillois and Baltrušaitis on these issues and, at the same time, discover an inextinguishable vein of human creative intelligence. Another parallel is the one created by Carl Gustav Jung in his *Libro Rosso* (Red book, 2010), where the active imagination and individuation are explored.

In the historical-stylistic framework set out in the preceding pages, Baltrušaitis, amid insights new and old, represents the importance of ambiguity within a system of emblems and symbols that underlies the kind of memory described above. With this idea in mind, we can identify the organic nature of an upended set of norms and the full legitimacy of a collection of anomalous and monstrous beauties rejected by humans especially in recent history. In his work Baltrušaitis has created a true celebration of wonder. Propelled by a delirium of the unusual and the unreal that has always bubbled up like a tempestuous passion in humanity, manifestations of sublime mastery appear before us: catoptric chambers, devices that transform men into animals, spheres of fire and prodigious halos, multiple suns, apparitions, duplications, aberrant perspectives, mutant physiognomies, stones decorated with figurative designs, mad gothic visions, and mysterious hieroglyphic emblems. The power of contemplated objects derives from a revisiting of an "alchemical alphabet" because the images studied express something more than the mere fact that they are illustrations or descriptions of elements and givens. By comparing art and nature, Baltrušaitis develops a cosmological theory based on a particular analysis of the forms of representation. As a result of their atemporal and universal consonance, "archetypes of the imagination" emerge in different cultures and traditions. Thus, the celebration of wonders provides a cluster of primitive and recurring depictions in which we see reflected the collective unconscious. Geometric patterns, vegetation, roots, minerals, and heavenly mechanisms are swept up in what may be termed an ontology of the different. Here, in the search for traits common to many exemplars, there is an emphasis on the represented object whose inner genius does not really reside in the intention of the artist or in the subject of the work or allegory but somewhere between the two. It is the genius of the landscape and the transformation it undergoes that tends to create a kingdom of supreme delights: a light, swift, and powerful spirit capable of founding the entire morphology of transformation, a daemon of invention that weaves alchemical paradigms. Artists and their audiences encounter each other in the aesthetic fascination that puts nature on display as it transforms it, tending toward both perfection and its opposite, both harmony and the breakdown of light and contours. The interplay between the exact sciences and fantasy in its pure state is reconstituted. Here, allegory, an instrument of a "monstrous" hermeneutics, dominates with its rich array of images.

Baltrušaitis provides us with a "monstrous hermeneutics," an outstanding work among the existing studies of ambiguity. This ontology of the different, as I have called it, also deals with the map of myths in the broadest sense of the term; for example, the myth of Isis, because this kind of study is similar to an "aberration" that gives rise to a map of forms and also acts as a point of reference for the optical illusion known as anamorphosis. We proceed, then, through various fields of knowledge and Egyptian theogonies to another point of perspectival distortion in an attempt to unveil metaphysical truths, truths associated with the esoteric and alchemical universe and imagined truths.

The network of relationships presented here concerns not only the domains of the fantastic but also those of seeing and appearing: of reality, illusion, and invention. Bernard Lassus has demonstrated this by highlighting on the level of landscape the transformation of the object when forms elude perception through the effect of camouflage. The acts of perceiving and imagining participate in an aesthetic game of mimetic simulation that involves exchanges and transformations. The "natural" image, like the technically reproduced one, is a mise en scène of the world.

The ensemble of wonders that Baltrušaitis (1973, 1978, 1999) offers us is the product of a light and airy but unsettling navigation. He depicts the opposite of the heavens, the other side of beauty. Caillois recalls this extravagant feat as he describes the nature of the emblem: citing *Réveils et prodiges* (Awakenings and wonders, 1960), he illustrates how Baltrušaitis examined, for example, the image of the Apocalypse, disconnecting it from the biblical account. The magical power of the biblical words is evident in the image's iterations, stretching from Heinrich Quentell's German Bible (1498) to the seventeenth-century frescoes at Mt Athos, and passing through Albrecht Dürer (1498) and the engravings of Jean Duvet (1561) along the way. Caillois claims that by doing what he did Baltrušaitis offers us a solitary and exciting reverie of the process of translation from one art form to another, a distancing full of nuances, a movement created by magical translations from literature to painting and from word to image. Thus, the iconographic transpositions change the meaning of the text in an aesthetic iridescence. This confirms the idea, mentioned above, of soaring creativity as the epitome of a "marvellous system of forms." Associated as they are to dreams, the oneiric, enigmatic, and bizarre, these expressions of the creative mind in essence pertain to the theory of iconic art developed by Horst Bredekamp (2015). This theory distinguishes between artifice (or the interplay of body and figuration) and the power of the form produced by the imagination in an intermediate work of "semantic plasticity" that reflects the perennial and stimulating contrast between matter and spirit.

Alongside the theme of the representation of nature and the nature of representation, we find the closely related themes of the opposite of the beautiful and of harmony. As Eugenio Battisti demonstrates, starting with the reflections and examples presented above, we cannot think the image in the fullest sense without a philosophy of representation that takes into account beauty, grace, and harmony, as well as their opposites.

2

Archetypes and the Evocation of Antiquity

What is an archetype? An original model, ideal structure, or primary image (or one considered so and irreplaceable), or a superior reality, or a thing at once a perfect specificity and universality, or, according to Carl Jung, an element of the collective unconscious. Archetypes are commonly found in myths and fables as well as in realist narratives; they are outside time, pre-exist sickness and pain, and display metamorphoses and rebirths. Their nature is a composite of culture, knowledge, magic, and dream.

Archetypes compel us to consider the relationships among the archaic, the sacred, and the sacred's eccentric opposite, the monstrous. The archaic designates the first or the most ancient of the art cycles. For the most part, the designation refers to the early Greek and Mediterranean civilizations, from the fifth century BCE onward. The archaic precedes the classical period, and its main features include religious inspiration associated with religious places, mythological stories, and narrative art. Johann Joachim Winkelmann's description of the characteristics of archaic art still rings true: namely, non-naturalistic motifs, stylization, imperfect or spontaneous imagery, and elements of clarity and repose (1980). Henri Focillon describes the archaic as not only an experimental stage in which style strives for definition but also as the charm of the wild, irrational, illogical, and non-imitative, something ingenuous and simultaneously monstrous, inexplicable, and magical in contrast to the profane (1987). Some interpreters identify in the sacred an absolute otherness accompanied by an ecstatic aesthetic response or feeling. We can, therefore, understand how, starting with invocation and evocation, certain categories can arise: the mystical, solemn, oneiric, marvellous, and visionary.

From the sacred's forms displayed in different styles in human storytelling, there emerges, in parallel to heart-warming beauty, the grotesque and the monstrous, in other words, the other face of the world. The archetype also raises a question relative to the various types of syncretism of cultures and traditions dispersed throughout history. Among these, Zolla discusses utopian syncretism, which help us to understand "neural networks" of human beings (1992, 59–66). He extols, in particular, the syncretism that developed in the course of the Florentine Renaissance (between 1439 and 1493) and contemporaneous Roman Renaissance, championed by Pomponio Leto and Platina (Giovanni Alvise Toscani), respectively. Syncretism enjoyed moments in the historical spotlight toward the end of the Byzantine Empire, as attested in the writings of Gemisthus Pletho (Plethon), an initiate of the philosophy of Elisseus and his school at Mystras. This is where the idea of the philosopher as "king of syncretistic thought" is formulated. Plethon – whose remains lie in the Malatesta Temple in Rimini, the interior reliefs of which are dedicated to the line of Zoroaster, Eumolpus, Minos, Lycurgus, Iphitus, and Numa, which connects Brahmins and Persian sorcerers with Curetes, Dodonians, Tiresias, and Chiron – supported the reconciliation of the Eastern and Western Churches. Basilios Bessarion, educated by Plethon, wrote his eulogy and then retired, after moving to the Church of Rome as cardinal titular of Santi Apostoli (Church of the Apostles). From here, along the path also taken by Nicholas of Cusa, we have the great teachings of Marsilio Ficino and Pico della Mirandola. The human spirit was illuminated by the fact that rational knowledge needed to be clarified in order for it to be identified with the ineffable mind of the cosmos; this could be achieved through contemplation, which, by bridging the gap between necessity and impossibility, provided the only access to being. This trajectory also includes a host of interpretations of Plato, in the form of esoteric readings that combine Christianity and Judaism. In Zolla's view wisdom converted life's bitterness and deception into consolation. It may be an apparition that could represent freedom from the ordinary world, such as the one that Artyom Solovyev had at the age of nine, when he experienced an ecstatic and revelatory vision of Sophia, or that of Pavel Florensky, for whom wisdom is the fourth hypostasis of God.

2 ANTIQUITY AS FUTURE

There are eternal returns in the history of art: antiquity, in particular, is a source of knowledge, a model, and a foundation for the future. It is also a project for the future, or antiquity itself may be experienced as the future, as Rosario Assunto writes in his study of neoclassical and early Romantic aesthetics and poetics (1973). The power of memory underpins the quality of innovations, authenticates novelty, and at times even generates provocations. Art is fundamentally permeated by antiquity, especially in the free play of fantastic forms and in the finest material products. Everything is a revision of visions, from the classicism of the Romans to the classicism of the age of Charlemagne, from humanism to the Enlightenment, from the resurgence of Renaissance elements in modernism to such resurgence in postmodernism. But originally the past was recreated by the Greeks in an "archaeology of nostalgia," to borrow John Boardman's phrase. Greek antiquity was steeped in myth, history, imagination, and personifications forming a dance of meanings and symbols. An archaic past circumscribed by a magical halo has always influenced the destiny of the present. Classicism evokes values considered to be universal, such as perfection, measure, equilibrium, harmony, grace, intensity of characteristic features, and naturalness. In this there is a future of the classical, according to Salvatore Settis, who examines the stages of the artistic civilization of the West. The more we are able to see the "classical" not as a dead inheritance that we possess without doing anything to merit it but as something surprising to rediscover each day, like a powerful stimulus to "understand" the different, the more we will be able to educate new generations for the future.

We need to deal with the fundamental aspects of this perspective by reflecting on the imagination and the grace of dreams in the ideative power of the relationship between art and nature, while providing appropriate examples. The notion of antiquity as future should be analyzed in the light of the modelling of reality into form and vice versa, without ignoring two different points of view useful for the objectives of the present book. The first is that of Georg Simmel, who, in the early twentieth century, claimed that the relative heights attained by technological progress had become an *absolute* value: the dazzle of technology combined with money was suffocating "spirituality" and "pensiveness," qualities that, in spite of degradation and the variability in tastes and conventions of the time, were succeeding nonetheless in offering their own particular response in the form of tension and nostalgia. The second viewpoint is that of Roland Barthes, who focuses on the endless resignification of the object observed, such that there is a permanent overflow of the senses with respect to first impressions. The real is enriched by the artificial. We might add, along with Hans Blumenberg, as regards what has come to be called "metaphorology," that myth implements a substratum by which the narrative is never only pure fantasy but rather the development of elementary templates: fantastical descriptions are essentially underpinned by mythological representations (2010, 107–21).

Let me be more specific by discussing the imagination and nature. If considered a kind of dream, the imagination sometimes allows us to gain access to the hidden order of a universal language that nature itself shapes and spontaneously articulates all around us, a language, we might say, of both nature and art, i.e., of being and doing, of the *poietic* arrangement of things and events. This is the case because nature pertains to art, the expression of living forms, and art pertains to nature, the expression of existent forms. The imagination is a language subject to the multiple and the changeable, as well as being shot through with myths and symbols, from given objects to metaphors, from truth to appearance and fictitiousness, from the ecstatic vision that the human being (as a part of nature, can have of it) to the illusions of a dream world. Multitudes of signs, symbols, and representations accompany us and seem to respond to us. But in what way? Is perceiving nature through an ecstatic gaze, insofar as it is the manifestation of an oneiric condition, an illusion that our mind needs, or is it related to an actual expression of things? Can the subjective element vanish in the oblivion of the self?

In seeking to respond to these questions, I would say that dreams are an experience that rescues us from the tyranny of time and space; it is an escape from the world while we still inhabit it. In this state we have the sensation of experiences rich in patterns, forms, and metaphors: images follow one another like the undulations of a melody. Indeed, we could say that we are enveloped in an ecstatic perception. This happens when something near us captures the attention of our gaze and induces us to imagine ourselves being observed by what we are in the act of contemplating. We learn to participate in a transformation: as I gaze at the trees, hills, valleys, mountains, and fields, everything that makes up the landscape comes nearer to me as if in a sort of fusion, act of love, and enchantment. I see myself everywhere. Distance is replaced by nearness. Perception has not changed into description but into illumination. This is the result of a sort of doubling of the object in which the visual field merges with the invisible and the dream takes up a position in the intervening space. As Giovanni Pascoli says in "Alexandros," "Dream is the infinite shadow of truth." Am I dreaming or am I awake? we sometimes say. This thought comes to us in the light of day and in the shadows situated between a dreamed world and a lived world, but even the lived world can be a dreamed world because the mind can abandon its control even in daytime and drift toward deeper realities. This is how art works.

For its part, nature has the capacity to appear before our eyes as either sleeping or illuminated, depending on its various personifications in Greek myth; this occurs precisely because it is concealed in the language of existing things, and because it seems to be possessed by a daemon that fixes and transforms places and humans. Through a surge of the imagination, we again find ourselves, as we contemplate it, in the grip of a *rhetoric of the ineffable*: an art of persuasion that seems to be lavished by nature itself in the time and space of its unfolding. Thus, magical charms motivate human beings in search of the truth beyond the appearances, starting with the enchantment of the earth with its sublime places, sacred mountains, grottoes, and springs. In this basically mystical perception, we can also sense, as Jean Richer claims, a certain mirroring effect between earth and sky. Like the Egyptians, the Greeks transformed their country into a living image of the sky in accordance with the constellations. They created a sacred geography within which Delphi, Sardis, and Delos appeared like the centres of three great signs of the zodiac, and this system of "planetary alignment" reflected the structure and location of the temple, the decoration of tympana and amphorae, for instance. In addition to the (ancient) image that I have called mystical, we also find another, which is useful for composing the perception of the landscape and of modern enigmatic nature. This process necessitates a full and new reading of mythology, and Reiner Maria Rilke's poetry illustrates this point well. Giorgio De Chirico's *Le Muse inquietanti* (The disquieting muses), Alberto Savinio's mythological masks, or Pablo Picasso's bulls and centaurs richly demonstrate this approach in painting, while the works of Jean Cocteau do so in film. The present returns to the past in order to embrace it as a model of the future.

By conjuring up apparitions and disappearances in the interchange between subject and object, the daemon in the secret language of nature activates the figures of the double vision. It is the force that penetrates both humans, with their representations, and nature, with its forms. This can be intuited in part by observing that certain images, which we perceive naturally, are in effect paintings even before they are painted; it is nature itself, in its various forms, that creates an infinite number of images. For some theorists, these images are in our mind prior to becoming actual artistic representations. Following from this idea, we can say that nature is the object of contemplation, inasmuch as it fades away, and of a mutual relationship between object and subject, because humankind appears to be possessed by the images that we ourselves naturally create under certain conditions. On the other hand, as we learn from David Freedberg, images are not limited to fixing themselves in our memory, but they predispose us to empathy or an endless interaction. They are linked to the passage from the visible to the invisible in the course of a "meditative" excursion, or a sort of enduring pause of the ecstatic-oneiric gaze. In ancient Greece, for example, as Károly Kerényi explains, vision and myth, and epiphany and mythology, cross-fertilized each other to create cultural images that articulated human archetypes, in other words, images that externalized the desire to become other figures. The theme around which the present discussion revolves is represented by the appearance and transformation of local gods. For ancient humans, nature is inhabited by gods and is transformed into a temple, as the temple is transformed into nature symbolically. Seeing was considered to be an obligatory stage in the journey toward the supernatural; there was a tight connection among place, vision, and the god who dwelt in the place. In short, to use one of Kerényi's own expressions, we find ourselves before what could be termed a transcendence of nature.

We have discussed the imagination, nature, and the daemon that dwells in the secret language of things, between the self and the object. We are now in a position to deal with the question of space. The historical relationship between places and deities is clear and serves to explain better the passage from the material to the non-material in the human being's encounter with nature. In the visionary experience of the appearance of things, the gesture of the gods is translated into poetic representations or pictorial depictions; this is because, through art, we rediscover the signs of that empathy mentioned above. As Claude Lévi-Strauss liked to repeat, the passage from nature to culture finds a privileged manifestation in art. The artistic condition originates in the dream of aesthetic intuition, in imagining the fantastic; at the same time, nature itself, as I have outlined, presents itself as an art form, and it does so in the guise of an "eloquent" arrangement of forms. A pleasant and necessary deceit enthralls the human being. We might add that the contemplation of nature is based on seeing the sacred whose meaning manifests itself symbolically, by means of objects and beings that become something totally other without ceasing to participate in their natural environments. This is Mircea Eliade's view: a sacred tree remains a tree even though it signifies something other than a tree, something from nature that is different from its nature as a tree. And so forth. For Eliade, the reality of the sacred is the invisible reality of the numinous, and because of this it is something ineffable. We are witness to an extended epiphany: the spontaneous environment, the seat of the gods, coexists with the productive environment of human beings. The language of nature is, therefore, an art of existing things that comes to life in representation, and dream corresponds to that art as illusion and revelation. This is what I called, two paragraphs above, the transcendence of nature.

We have spoken of the naturalization of art, the transcendence of nature within temporality, and the need to rediscover ancient ways of thinking and doing aesthetically. As noted, this occurred in various historical periods, in the form of the revival of classical ideas, from medieval allegories to the mythographies of humanism; then in the twentieth century we saw examples of oneiric art inspired by these motifs. As Stefano Benassi points out, the ancients are the foundation of the modern, which can be seen in the aesthetic models we find in literature and the figurative arts. Jacques Derrida reminds us of the importance of the act of painting for human experience, because in painting a form of recognition is projected as a remembering that activates a performative and not simply representative or descriptive act that creates an endlessly renewed event. For this reason, art relies on memory, constitutes itself, and recognizes itself in a process of constant self-renewal.

Finally, at the end of the twentieth century, and especially in these last few years of the new millennium already dominated by citationism, we have two more important cases that illustrate how an earlier image can enrich the suggestiveness of the present image. In the last phase of the postmodern, there is a kind of return to the past that takes it as a template for the future. We find it in many of Bill Viola's video installations, which borrow elements from the frescoes of Masolino da Panicale, Pontormo, and Paolo Uccello, as well as Lech Majewski's film (*The Mill and the Cross*, 2011), inspired by Peter Bruegel the Elder's *Ascent to Calvary* and a modern interpretation of redemption. This demonstrates eloquently the presence of antiquity, with its many expressive forms, in contemporary art.

3 THE THEME OF THE INEFFABLE AND THE VISION OF THE ROMANTICS

After the crisis of the Enlightenment and end of the French Revolution, the image of the divine reappears in European art but without the celebration of the dogmas of established religion. The first half of the nineteenth century is imbued with a sense of the infinite that inspires a veritable poetics of the sacred. Essentially, the Romantic writer or artist once again experiences the presence of God in a profoundly intimate way, along with that of Satan, and with nothingness. The daemon of spirituality in fact expands the boundaries of the sacred to include its darker and more troubling aspects. Writers, artists, and musicians are driven in their spiritual aspiration by what various scholars refer to as "negative theology." Many Romantics, therefore, could identify with the thinking of Giacomo Leopardi, who writes, "In short, the principle of all things, and indeed of God, is nothingness" (*Zibaldone* [Notebook], 18 July 1821). The source of this kind of reflection is ancient, dating back as it does to Neoplatonism and particularly

Plotinus, whose varied influence on the Romantics is well established. But I do not wish to talk about Neoplatonism as it relates to the topic of this book, but rather about myth and symbolism. I would point out that in the Romantic movement art itself was created and received as something sacred, and whose conceptual, ritualistic, and representational structures Giorgio Agamben (*Homo sacer*) discusses masterfully. Jean-Marie Schaeffer also deals with this issue in *The Art of the Modern Age*, highlighting its ecstatic quality, especially in Germany, among idealist philosophers and Romantic artists. Schopenhauer, who called himself an enthusiastic follower of Kant, speaks of the metaphysics of the beautiful.

In general, the domain of the sacred, which encompasses the ineffable, unsayable, and inexplicable, celebrates an uncommon, exceptional, and inviolable experience: the relationship with the divine. A preliminary way of understanding the sacred is through contrast: the sacred contrasts with the profane, as the pure contrasts with the impure. The closer we come to the sacred, the more we drift away from the world. This is the characteristic feature of what is separate but that exists in the contact with the divine and the manifestation of its power. Involved here is a force that human beings project outside themselves, objectifying it, and that they subsequently intuit in order to experience it as "external" and uncontrollable. It is possible to connect these issues with aspects of Romantic sensibility and imagination. We note an important change: the object of inspiration and representation is no longer faith but the evocation of its form. The sacredness of aesthetic intuition or, in a bold inversion, the sacred itself as aesthetic intuition, represents a radical turn. Art shapes ritual, recreates the power of its sublime object, and reveals its secret daemon. By drawing nourishment from the imaginary of religions and myths, art becomes Art; it envelops itself in a divine aura and acquires an oracular quality. As the universe of feelings, the entire world passes through this aura as it becomes its absolute interpreter. The Romantics erect a special altar for art in a very secret place, in the *temenos* (a piece of land marked off from common use) of creative inspiration. The

Romantic age instituted a devotion to the beauty of nature and the experience of ecstatic states. In his *Lectures on Aesthetics* Georg Wilhelm Friedrich Hegel captures the spirit of that process in an important passage, which reads, "Art reveals *the divine*, the most profound interests of humanity, and the most comprehensive truths of the mind" (1997, 12; translated by Corrado Federici). In order to understand better this relationship, however, we need to go beyond the Hegelian view of knowledge that concerns art, religion, and philosophy.

As one possible point of comparison between French and Italian authors and philosophers influenced by the vitality and originality of German and English culture, the theme of the sacred in eighteenth- and nineteenth-century aesthetics revolved around the development of the concepts of symbol and mythology. Through the efficacy of the imagination, philosophical reflections on poetics and art theory proceeded together in an effort to affirm the invisible spirit of nature and in the process introduced a new conception of the relationship between the human and the divine. This development entailed a coming together of artistic and speculative creativity, on the one hand, and religion, on the other – a fusion that assumes the form of mystery and prophecy. This was the new domain of the marvellous, which evoked the Middle Ages through the "supernatural," an imaginary populated by wizards, demons, knights, saints, and heroes that removes myths from established religions and history and preserves their autonomy in thought and sensibility.

The Romantics and their precursors saw in the sacred, associated with the feeling for myth and nature, a menacing attraction, dangerous energy, and indistinct and disturbing aura, as Caillois clearly points out in *Man and the Sacred*.

During the seventeenth century, in the face of the decline and the ruin of religion, the rehabilitation of myth got underway, promoting an intense participation in the world, with its energies and its primitive language (word and chant). Isaac Vossius and Giambattista Vico noted this development, while Jean-Jacques Rousseau and Johann Gottfried Herder reflected on its theoretical implications. The new awareness lent legitimacy to myths on both the ontological and the poetic levels, turning attention to diverse primitive literatures (the *Edda*, Ossian, the sacred books of the Orient, the chants of the Native Americans). A new and irresistible feeling achieved fullness in the evocation of remote and primitive historical periods. Ancient Nordic and oriental lore was superimposed on Homer, Aeschylus, Pindar, and Virgil, generating in the process a passion sublime, enormous, wild, vivifying, and overwhelming.

At the start of the eighteenth century, myth, mere ornament with profane features, becomes the sacred par excellence: the revelatory aspects of fables. The sacred recuperates a psychological function, on the one hand, and human faculties and collective actions are enhanced, on the other (consider the rehabilitation of the sacred in France's revolutionary-era festivals). In the eighteenth century, as Jean Starobinski informs us in *Teoria del simbolo* (Theory of the symbol), the sacralization of myth is intimately linked with the humanization of the sacred. From this double transformation emerges a new antithesis of the sacred and the profane. Myth is no longer a theogony but an anthropogony. A de-aestheticizing of theology correlates to the sacralizing of aesthetics, as many argue.

4 ON THE WINGS OF THE SYMBOL

The sacred attracts our attention because it relates to the development of categories of taste. Even though linked to beauty and grace as a manifestation of the divine, it is different from them. It is possibly something more powerful and more profound. The sacred may contain tragic elements, but the oracular theme of the temple god and the inescapability of human destiny contrast with its splendid pacifying image: emotional tumult finds quiet and comfort there. It is similar to the sublime, but it does not convey the unconscious dimension of that "elevated feeling," neither in Nicolas Boileau and his followers, nor in Edmund Burke and his; nor is it particularly appropriate for neoclassicists or lovers of gothic ruins and landscapes. The sacred is permeated by elements of this aspect of taste without being identical with it. From the standpoint of aesthetics, the sacred is neither a "disquieting Muse" nor terror. Reducible to neither a dignified oration nor the sweetness of grace, it is not a requirement of perfection or harmony; it is not a variant of *je ne sais quoi*, i.e., something that emanates a mysterious, indefinable charm, nor a product of rules, of elegance without affectation, or of the attraction of surprise tied to individual experience (in the manner of ideas advanced by Dominique Bouhours, Pierre de Marivaux, and the Baron de Montesquieu). The sacred generates a feeling of wonder in the presence of the cosmos, earth, and elements, but also in the presence of the promptings of tradition, myth, and the human spirit. The Romantics communicated the revelation of the numinous through a variety of manifestations, from extraordinary apparitions to wonders that unfold in the intuitive faculties and in the aesthetic life: the Romantics were at times literally possessed by them. The sacred was no longer a feature of religion but the feeling for beauty that includes art, nature, and faith. We are not dealing with a category of the indefinable and the individual but a feeling for the ineffable and the universal. The sacred, then, is a utopia of revelation, the search for a mysterious, secret aura. For these reasons it can give rise to a feeling of excitation. We are able to discover Art and the Absolute in the anguish of an enchantment.

Concerning the religious approach in strict terms, I would like to point out that some (e.g., Balthasar 1975–86) speak of a "theological aesthetics," referring to the great change that occurred in the interconnections between philosophy, art, and religion in German idealism and Romanticism. More specifically, the crux of the issue developed around the relationship between the Bible and aesthetics during a time of secularization. In the confluence of Christian revelation and the doctrine of the beautiful, an exponent of theological aesthetics, Johann Georg Hamann, was the first, at that time, to sketch out a doctrine of worldly and pagan beauty together with Christian beauty. We should also mention Johann Gottfried Herder and the conjunction of poetry and theology in his work. In *The Spirit of Christianity* (1797), and before that in *Another Philosophy of History for the Education of Humanity* (1776), he states that there exists an organic link between divine inspiration and the human capacity for inspiration, and he discusses the excitement of an authentic awakening that originates in God. Like many of his era, he is influenced by a pantheistic vision that humanizes Christianity by amalgamating the natural and the supernatural.

François-René de Chateaubriand's *The Genius of Christianity* (1802) has spiritual origins like those of Herder's "aesthetic Christianity." It stands against reason and in favour of sentiment and the imagination. Operating in the climate of classicism and German idealist Romanticism, Herder takes a position between aesthetic humanism and Christianity. Chateaubriand, for his part, retains Christianity and its dogmas as he describes the charm that emanates from the Christian mysteries, as well as Christianity's impact on art and thought; he also discusses its marvellous ornaments, liturgies, and rituals. In Hans Urs von Balthasar's analysis, based on a theological critique, Herder is a theologian and aesthetician, whereas Chateaubriand is an aesthetic apologist.

In a dizzying array of images, the genius of Christianity is the genius of the Romantic spirit in the presence of which the philosophy of history is wrapped in the veil of a restorative nostalgia. In *The Genius of Christianity*, Chateaubriand exalts French seventeenth-century literary tradition by reading history within the frame of religious feeling. He is the first to interpret that tradition as manifestly Christian literature. Considered are the writings of Blaise Pascal, Jacques-Benigne Bossuet, and Jean de La Bruyère; however, that mystical flower of seventeenth-century literature, that fascination with the inner world, from François de Sales to François Fénelon (and including Pierre de Bérulle, Jean-Pierre Camus, Louis Lallemant, Jean-Jacques Olier, Jean Joseph Surin, and Jean de Bernières-Louvigny) had long wilted by Chateaubriand's time. Its last protagonist was Jean-Pierre Caussade (1675–1751). We might also add, at the end of the eighteenth century, the name of Louis Claude de Saint-Martin, who was influenced by Jacob Böhme.

Our discussion of the theme developed here also includes the term *marvellous*. Chateaubriand speaks of the "Christian marvellous," citing Dante, Torquato Tasso, and John Milton, by which he meant the capacity to represent the supernatural, i.e., angels, demons, and the kingdoms of the world beyond. In his *Lettera semiseria di Grisostomo* (Half-serious letter from Chrysostom to his son, 1816), Giovanni Berchet identifies the terrifying and horrific Nordic legends as the source of Romantic poetry. Ermes Visconti (*Idee elementari della poesia romantica* [Basic ideas concerning Romantic poetry], 1818) sees the marvellous as the most typical feature of Romantic aesthetics and locates it in tales of witches and oddities such as we might find in oriental literatures. Madame de Staël (*De la littérature* [Of literature], 1800, and *De l'Allemagne* [Of Germany], 1813) points out the ghosts in Ossian's poems and praises Rousseau, Bernardin de Saint-Pierre, Edward Young, and Thomas Gray; more than the marvellous, she defends the supernatural, referring to the witches and ghosts in Shakespeare, along with their absorbing effects. This is an emotionalism that blends forward-looking elements and melancholy. All these themes converge to create a complex picture that leads back into the imaginary of the sacred.

In his *Philosophy of Art* (1802–03), Friedrich Wilhelm Joseph Schelling considers the marvellous as a truly novel feature of the modern Christian epic as compared to the ancient epic. With Christianity and the separation of the divine from the earthbound, the marvellous enters human history like the intervention of the Absolute.

In France, with the advent of the Enlightenment, mystical spirituality faded into the background, while in the second half of the eighteenth century, reason ceased to be the faculty that leads to the transcendent. Opponents of the Enlightenment included Joseph de Maistre, a critic of modern thought, inspired, in his own words, by the negative principle of a "theophobia," and Maine de Biran, a major representative of the revival of spiritualism with his doctrine of introspection. This was also the time of the repudiation of Franz Anton Mesmer's teachings (in 785), and of Emanuel Swedenborg's, whose work would be later admired by Samuel Taylor Coleridge and Charles Baudelaire, among others. Some years later, in 1810–12, Georg Friedrich Creuzer (*Simbolica e mitologia* [Symbolism and mythology],

2004) would be criticized for describing mythology as a documentation of humanity's absolute wisdom; he denounces modern culture for its inability to appreciate the connection between the sacred and the human, which had been enriched by antiquity through the mystical and Dionysian experiences. For Creuzer, only the symbol can reveal that nexus, which emerges from the depths of being, offering an instantaneous visual perception of phenomenal reality and its metaphysical foundations. The excesses of Enlightenment rationality brought about the loss of the symbolic faculty.

The principal themes of Romantic aesthetics converge on the notion of the symbol. As Tzvetan Todorov (1984) explains, the symbol has an inexhaustible quality, revealing the unsayable and expressing itself both directly and indirectly. It is an image. To be clear, August Wilhelm Schlegel, citing Schelling, claims that the "the beautiful is a symbolic representation of the infinite" (36; translated by Corrado Federici). The infinite can be brought to the surface only symbolically. The symbol is not a function of abstract reason; it is, instead, an intuitive and perceptible way of grasping things. According to hermetic doctrine, art, as symbolic form, possesses a privileged access to the absolute, the universal; it tends toward ideas in their visible reality; it is able to capture the ideal and universal aspect concealed in every perceptible form. The task of art is to provide universal forms that are simultaneously ideal and real. Such forms are called ideas or, using an unusual term, *gods*. The gods are real, living, existing ideas; therefore, the manifestation of universal ideas as real is given to us by mythology. The Schlegel brothers also evoked a kind of new mythology as the hieroglyphic expression of nature that provides the conscious mind with the enjoyment of contemplation.

The sacred presupposes a poetics of the ineffable, something that is untranslatable. Art expresses something that cannot be said in any other way. The ineffable is clearly present in certain works of Romantic literature, painting, and music. Many writers and artists solve the problem by resorting to images: the sacred cannot be spoken, but it can be represented. Poetry conveys the unsayable through several aesthetic devices provided by rhetoric and issued from the imagination. Poetic language (the art of language) thus generates within us a plurality of interrelated sensations The ineffable is expressed by this plurality, carried on the wings of the symbol. Wilhelm Heinrich Wackenroder argued very effectively in favour of the notion of art as the expression of the invisible using a marvellous language. More generally, for the Romantics, dealing with the divine also means concealing the principle of things. As Todorov explains, in reference to Friedrich Schlegel, "the divine cannot be expressed except allegorically, precisely because it is inexpressible. Symbolism as a whole is a principle of poetry. The divine can be spoken of only indirectly. We cannot express God in art except symbolically" (1984, 283; translated by Corrado Federici).

When we say that the work of art alludes to the infinite, we are really saying that the sacred originates in the representation and symbolism of the ineffable. This is how the sacred, the sense of the divine, makes itself perceived or felt.

We therefore find the secret of the sacred in all this. With this vision, the Romantics created an aesthetic celebration, a solemn oration that illustrates the transfer of the treasure of religion into its own spirit: free of dogmas, rich in beauties that it accumulates and makes its own, like a precious trove; thus, the Romantic spirit throws itself into a cosmic embrace without precepts, attaining in the process a new form of enchantment, a new marvellous, and a new kind of consolation.

5 ANAMNESIS OF THE VISIBLE: THE PLAY OF THE ARTS

We now need to consider the historical period – but which history, the factual or the psychological? The spirit of our age is a history of facts, but it is also a history of interiority, as we learn from Edgar Morin. Art and aesthetics, however, walk a tightrope over the void, and they do so with a special sensibility. Speaking of the "necessity of art" and of nihilism, Sergio Givone identifies three important figures: the aesthete, the dandy, and the flâneur, each of whom suffers from a particular kind of schizophrenia:

> They profess an uncompromising nihilism and yet joyfully attend to the spectacle of the world. They do not believe in anything but have the gift of casting upon things a gaze that animates and illuminates them. And while they know how to immerse themselves in every situation and live it personally, an incurable solitude keeps them removed from the thing that seems to make them tremble. They are musical creatures; as Søren Kierkegaard, Oscar Wilde, and Baudelaire would observe, they especially feel the rhythm, the internal melody, of the events that attract them and are immediately in tune with these elements. But by the same token they de-realize and dissolve specific contents with the result that their social status is sabotaged and they become alien, incomprehensible, or suspicious beings. Each of them attempts to escape from this conflict in his own way: the aesthete through irony, the dandy by disguising himself, and the flâneur by turning himself into a thing (1995, 107; translated by Corrado Federici).

These three emblematic figures preserve the memory of nothingness, of origins, and of personal identity.

Whether believable or not, the visible, defined in these terms, can also be expressed by the most recent technology through the image that Ian McEwan offers of it in his 2019 novel *Machines Like Me*, which revolves around the relationship between a man, woman, and android. Essentially, the implied question here is whether we as a species are being made completely robotic, on our way to being bio-engineered artificial humans, as in an updated version of Ridley Scott's iconic 1982 film, *Blade Runner*.

Anamnesis of the visible may be understood either as the medical history of a patient or as a recollection in the Platonic sense, where real knowledge emerges from memory or, in the case of the visible, as a recollection of ideas or forms that the soul knew while residing in the eternal realm. As regards visual and plastic forms, we can think of the essence behind appearances. We bring to bear both modes of perception, adapting them to the substance of mental images and figurative design of paintings – and, by extension to the arts in general, as Jean-François Lyotard suggests (1998, 1–8) – to the signs of a gesture within matter. The "visual gesture" generally concerns what is optical, but it can also become an event in the Freudian sense, revealing what is hidden or what is repressed. At stake here is the truthfulness of the subject represented and of its concealments. Proceeding along this line of reasoning, we access art's metaphorical nature, its use of figures in a rhetorical-linguistic process. The space opened up by the data present in visual representation tends to evoke, restore, or make us relive the element that consciousness does not grasp or want to grasp: something related to the *aura* (in the sense Walter Benjamin used it, that is, as an effect of an original artwork, which is lost when that artwork is reproduced) or to the attraction of something that is absent but that we would like to disguise. From this, the importance of internal and external images, which Antonio Prete highlights (2016), clearly emerges. The anamnesis of the visible is therefore transversal because it captures a chain of associations that cannot be conceptualized only as the past or as a concrete given insofar as it exists in an intermediate state, without memory and not really presentable. Yet it has a significance of its own, despite the fact that it cannot find a place in which to inscribe itself concretely. Anamnesis cannot be ascertained by starting with the checkerboard of mental data; the visible is largely elusive. Discerning its hidden nature, therefore, depends on its plane or level of representation and our interpretative approach; a map or a diagram is different from a painting, a photograph, a film sequence, or a digital image. It is true that writing and painting provide images and therefore representations, but they do so in terms that are specific to their language, i.e., words, forms, and colours. From the Lascaux cave paintings to the paintings of a Cézanne or a Picasso, a space-time is created by the play of appearances and concealments. Perhaps the artistic gesture is like a spasm, a contraction of instants of attention, an active agency that radiates tactility and leaves an imprint to be deciphered in terms of the recognizable and the unrecognizable: it has to do with both the aesthetic act and the artistic act. It is, perhaps, this spasm of creativity that awakens in the reader or the viewer the spirit of the object presented, a sweet trauma of illumination and essence. As a result of this gesture, namely, the spasm of creativity, there exists the image that causes the object to appear in an interplay of appearances and disappearances. In the almost countless poietic practices throughout history, there opens up a whole field of almost clinical studies of aesthetics that becomes, in the words of Lyotard, a concrete ontology of *aistheton* (what is perceived by the senses). This spirit of representation is embodied in a celebratory system that coincides with the establishment of the academies of art, art collections, museums, and archives, as the memory and recognition of the Enlightenment-era and, later, Romantic-era middle class. For that social class, "representing" meant making visible reality come alive as an object to be appropriated, along a trajectory that extended from Neoplatonic memory, through the fifteenth-century theory of perspective, to modern mechanics, optics, and physics, thereby ensuring the intelligibility of the world. Meanwhile, the avant-gardes, which are contemporaneous with the crisis of reason in physics and mathematics in the early twentieth century, as well as a concomitant crisis of ethical values, revealed to us the agony of humanism and its spirit. The system was held captive by economic development and the limitless capacity for technical reproduction in a continuous display of disfigurements. In this process traditional works and those of the avant-garde became interesting in the context of human development but only within the production economy and culture industry. In the last few years, representation as a trace of the artistic gesture risks being deprived of its authentic value as free play of the imagination, to be replaced by what Jean Baudrillard (1981) calls its simulacrum in the virtual society. As regards the trauma of sensibility in the present day, and, at the same time, the perversion of contemplation, we may well wonder about the nature of harmony.

6 AURAS OF GRACE

When we look at human society in all its variety, we realize that there is a whole host of correspondences among cultures, arts, forms of knowledge, and languages: human society is a perennial, dynamic phenomenon that has unfolded over the course of time. This image of interconnections arises spontaneously with the first impression offered by material forms and representations, be they real or imaginary objects. Expressivity and meaning making are the result of their existence, in that they are images of space and in space. Our gaze naturally follows the articulated path created by empirical givens and signs capable of producing a diegetic creation, in other words, promoting the weaving of a narrative in which the languages of the plastic arts and the verbal arts converge. The gaze temporalizes space and spatializes time. It does this, we might say, "naturally" through what is called mythopoeia, an invented narrative that works in concert with the abilities of individuals and the practices performed on the level of qualia or the subjective component of sense perception (see Aristotle's *Categories*), which determine the acts of producing and the evoking as well as matter and words. All artistic systems have arrayed at their disposal the phenomenal entities that they utilize in specific situations. The priority of the play of qualia is what, in Aristotelian terms, could be called the perceptible that is proper to each art (*idion aistheton* and *oikeion ergon*).

We realize that we *read* the forms of architecture in the flow of time, just as we *see* the images of things whose meaning is determined by the written text, in an inner virtual space. In their search for a commonality among the different arts, some thinkers have tried to apply the convention of notation, using music as an analogy, while others have looked at the problem of aesthetic invariance (as all the arts are arts if they correspond to poetry, according to Benedetto Croce, or if they correspond to music, according to Schopenhauer). Still others, for example, Abraham Moles, have emphasized, in their study of lived space, the idea of a kind of "mental map" that is constitutive of the image of the world in each of us. But, in this case, the analogous subject is the spirit of narration itself, which is to say, the narrating soul of what appears in our artificer gaze before and after it has produced the work; as Roland Barthes (1985) and, along similar lines, Gérard Genette ([1966–72] 1969–76) have pointed out, the gaze is associated with duration and is situated in an "overflow" zone. Endowed with a special resonance, the image expands in a halo of signification. Furthermore, the gaze accompanies the gesture that it creates via intervals, pauses, empty spaces, as it weaves connective strands between acoustic and visual signals, as André Leroi-Gourhan (1993, 1:187–209) points out in his study of preliterate symbolic thought as well as the general thought of his own contemporary period. The gaze, then, be it projective or descriptive, will always be narrative.

If we compare artistic "languages," we clearly note that Gotthold Ephraim Lessing's distinction between the temporal and the spatial arts is superseded because it is too antiquated, schematic, and is inadequate for describing the transformations and inter-connections in the arts. We therefore need to place ourselves in the intermediate zone, that is, in the gaze that is situated between time and space, and to see architecture as a material, presentative art, and literature as a non-material, representational art. The difference resides in the qualia (the qualitative properties of sub-jective experience), which distinguishes them, does not negate a certain similarity on the level of narration. According to Plotinus (*Enneads*), architecture is the building without the stones. This is a very interesting idea. But we cannot entirely accept this obser-vation because it would mean disregarding experience in that the only way to understand the statement is to use words to describe the distribution of the parts of the structure relative to the structure as a whole, or its lightness or weight: this emphasis on the experiential is what permits us to distinguish between description of a particular art object and Art in the abstract, in order to give to the different arts what differentiates them and to Art what remains. Jean-Paul Sartre (*What Is Literature?*) observes that the art of prose is executed on a material that gradually becomes naturally signifying: words are not objects but they designate objects. Prose is an attitude of the spirit; and it is prose when, says Paul Valéry, the word passes through our gaze "comme passe le verre au travers du soleil" (like the sun passes through glass). And now we are at the heart of the matter; that is to say, we are inside language the way we are inside our bodies; we feel and perceive the body just as we feel and perceive language and the world. This is because the word is a moment of action and, I might add, a narrative action. And what remains of the material arts and discourses is the act, either the aesthetic act, according to Baldine Saint Girons, or the artistic act. Also worth pointing out here is the need to involve an array of correspondences, which comparative aesthetics has identified as one of its disciplinary tasks (Souriau 1985). Originally, in prose writing, the aesthetic act coexists with the execution of the artistic act; thought in action, gesture that measures, organizes, and assembles in sequences or complex associations. The figure of the creator-artist, essentially evoked here, often appears in ancient Greek texts. We should also apply the words *poiesis* and *poietes*, generally referring to the created object and the creator, to poetry and the poet in the technical sense.

Souriau's reference was chosen for the purpose of shedding light on an aspect of doing, and what is of interest, in the present context, is the poiesis that is common to both arts (i.e., architecture and literature), and not so much the element that aims at the universal good and the beautiful.

The memory of this disappears in the evident; the language of the qualia forgets and veers away from its philosophical foundation, and it has been this way from Marius Pollio Vitruvius to Frank Gehry. Memory does not, however, dissolve; rather, it conceals itself to then reappear. This also applies to the novel. Memory is anaphoric, especially in aesthetics and art. Materials, things, forms, and words produce images. We try to identify images in sequences and organize them in multiple networks in conformity with a plan, schema, project, or flash of insight. In this adventure of doing-seeing-narrating, we ourselves are nature in nature, and this relationship cannot be dissolved. In whatever way we create, we naturalize; in whatever way we are naturalized, we create. Every act suggests a doing that is conditioned by the act of imagining, thinking, and planning in an unending process. And there is no poiesis without *phantasia* (as we find in Plato). We rely on symbolic thought and the spirit of wandering in the practice of the perceptible and the experiential. The ontology of doing is reflected in an ontology of representing and vice versa: patterns of material and non-material interventions alternate with the physiology of the emotions. In the intermediate zone, where the ontologies meet and lose their distinguishing features, architecture and literature display their genius by integrating themselves in common reality, turning themselves into things and worlds that are not deliberately conspicuous and foundational in the aesthetic and artistic acts, so that the metaphor itself is lively and productive. This is the "auratic" route to finding oneself, to giving space, and to making space, so that the presentative aspect of architecture is not detached from its belonging to the world and from its capacity to represent. Space is space inhabited by the narrative of objects, forms, and people in a "domestic" perceiving; architecture, therefore, displays a narrative web and so it approaches literature, an approach that is participation in the narrative, the myth, and the living being.

But what is behind the aesthetic question of the interrelations among the arts, their systems, and their poetics? Why does an invisible thread bind them to cultures, forms of knowledge, and thoughts created in different countries, continents, and populations of the earth throughout history, and what does this invisible thread, which is important to the perception of nature and art in its various expressions, consist of? It is not so much a matter of the individual values of culture that I want to highlight as I imagine the future of art, or of a possible next system of the arts and their classifications. Rather, it is a matter of understanding the mental paradigm that allows us to comprehend, in the course of time and in the intersection of different cultures, the aesthetic act and the artistic act in which the paradigm assumes tangible form, which is to say, the synesthetic metaphor. From the various studies in comparative aesthetics and transcultural aesthetics in the Anthropocene and now the Novacene epochs, which make it possible for us to see and to compare the expressive development of many cultural factors and traditions, we need to extract, above all, a methodology. In fact, we need to follow the study of distinct phenomena, each separated from the others by time and space, and to distance ourselves from the exoticism that attracts us with forms of expression and a civilization that are foreign to us, an attraction that idolizes a distant land. Toward the end of the last century, intellectuals and philosophers developed, instead, a comparative aesthetic reflection that attempted to avoid preferring one part of the world to another.

7 THE ENIGMA OF THE UNSAYABLE

After examining the arts from a comparative perspective and engaging in a broader analysis of the poetics and art in our lives, we could say, along with Schopenhauer, that we are not intellect alone, according to the European philosophical model. If we were, we would step outside of the phenomena, appearances, and illusions that are reflections of ourselves and that offer themselves to us in the form of an external representation of consciousness. We are also body, the will to live that sees through experience to intuit its essence: things are the objectification of the will to live. Dealing with representations in the context of a comparative aesthetics establishes the positionality of the subject. From the theme of similarity or difference between a painting and a sculpture, a sonnet and an amphora, an architectural project and a piece of music, as discussed earlier, we now proceed to examining the dynamic semantic spectrum of the beautiful in ideas, feelings, and forms while keeping in mind both postmodernism and modernization. The forms in the aesthetic and artistic act can evoke absence or presence, pleasure or displeasure. It is not always the case that everything is present or identifiable in a work or an image; there is also something important or hidden that we miss. At the same time, it is not always the case that reading or viewing is a pleasant experience because something unpleasant can strike and jar our sensibility. If we compare the languages of reading and viewing, words create a semantic field that here and there appears to be underlying, implicit, or concealed. What holds all this together? In the previous section, I mentioned the activity of the synesthetic metaphor, the foundation of the entire comparative system. Out of this activity there arises the wonder of knowledge and the beauty of forms. And this metaphoric state exists on three levels, which are interconnected: pathways and cognitive experiences, languages, and artistic techniques. The key terms are poiesis, or human making of objects and the objects in representation, *aisthesis*, or the apparatus of emotions and feeling, and *theoria*, or the detachment of the senses which results in the act of contemplation. Synesthetic metaphors operate in the language of the human mind. Metaphors are tropes that exist between truth and imitation, between the expressible and the unsayable. We can also find them in the Indian aesthetic theory of flavours (*rasa*), and in the values of the void as expressed in the canons of Chinese and Japanese art. They propose gradations of representation that convey emotions. The synesthetic metaphor is the point where knowledge, sensibility, and contemplation converge; the representing gesture originates perceptually in contemplation. It is a mental construct based on sensations; it echoes the world, orchestrates symbols and analogues, controls feeling and imagining, and coordinates the correspondences among things. It is an abbreviated simile that transfers meanings and activates synecdoche and metonymy, i.e., the part for the whole or its opposite, the effect for the cause or its opposite. Several scholars have emphasized the great importance of the synesthetic metaphor, which is the foundation of both the aesthetic act and the artistic doing because of the affective, psychological, and personal power it entails. The phrase "the flowers speak and the air is white," from Honoré de Balzac's *Seraphita* (1834, 69), complements the present discussion and illustrates the point. We can find this metaphor in many works of literature, even in far-flung cultures. Those who underscore its importance include Henri Focillon, in *The Life of Forms* (1942); Erwin Panofsky, in *Studies in Iconology* (1962); and Ernst Gombrich, in *Art and Illusion* (1965) and, later, *The Sense of Order* (1979). In the sixties and seventies, especially in the fields of linguistics, rhetoric, and semiotics, we have the studies of Gérard Genette (*Figures*, [1966–72] 1969–76), Albert Henry (*Metonymy and Metaphor*, 1971), Roman Jakobson (*Questions de poétique* [Questions of poetics], 1973), and Roland Barthes, with his notions of the "halo" and "signification" (in "Straight in the Eye," 1977). This last work enables us to make an important comparison with the idea of resonance in the Indian concept of *dhvani* (sound), where the fascination of the word and the image associated with it exists somewhere between memory and expectation. We appear to have a precise description of this from Ananda K. Coomaraswamy, a universalist interpreter of Hinduism and Buddhism. In *Hinduism and Buddhism* (1943), after asserting that Buddha has discovered the way to eliminate suffering by teaching humans to suppress their individuality in order to achieve access to the entirety of reality, which is endless becoming, he offers the reader an interesting comparison of the power of appearance that is in line with what has been said here. In this regard Coomaraswamy (1987, 95) cites as a distant comparator Plato's *Protagoras*, "to be overcome by pleasure means just this – ignorance in the highest degree" (357e); and he comments as follows: "This letting oneself go is ignorance, while control of oneself is certainly wisdom (*sophia*, and in Pāli *kusalata*)." Consequently, the power of appearances (*tō phainomenon*, and in Pāli *rupa*) "causes us to wander in confusion" (356d). This means that the beginning of wisdom is the end of desires. But on the theme of wisdom, in the face of the world that reveals itself, which is the other side of appearances, he also states, again citing Plato (*Theaetetus*, 155d) and Aristotle (*Metaphysics* I, 2 982b, 2), that wisdom begins with wonder. Wonder, therefore, accompanies the first instance of knowledge. In Hindu culture, one of the fullest elaborations of the idea of the world as expression of the divine is Vasugupta's *Aphorisms of Shiva* (2013) (from the ninth century, with commentary by Rajanaka Ksemaraja in the tenth and eleventh centuries). Here, we read something extraordinary related to dreams, reality, and the imagination:

> Like the sense of wonder felt by one who experiences
> something out of ordinary experience, so too the feeling
> of wonder, in intense enjoyment, *Abhoga*, of our contact with
> the various manifestations of knowable reality, is continually

produced, in this great *yogin* with the entire wheel of the senses, increasingly unfurled, motionless, fully disclosed, by virtue of the penetration of its most intimate nature, compact unity of consciousness and always new, extreme, extraordinary wonder (*camatkara*). The stages of yoga are a wonder. (Vasugupta 2013, 126; translated by Corrado Federici)

The spirit of Indian art and its representation appear to correspond to Schopenhauer's concept of will and representation.

In his study "Immagini della natura nella poesia indiana classica" (Images of nature in classical Indian poetry, 2017), Giuliano Boccali writes that the poetry of India was hailed by European intellectuals at the end of the seventeenth century as "nature poetry." In 1791, a year prior to the first German translation of Kalidasa's drama *Shakuntala*, which appeared two years after William Jones's English translation, Goethe expressed his admiration in verses that convey impressions of totalities like the sky and the earth (Goethe 1983). The Romantics generally emphasized the power of natural imagery as a cultural topos that, however, seems as much Indian as it does European. For ancient India, learning to observe aesthetically is part of a canon or a tradition. Boccali points out that, in *Shakuntala*, as in all classical Indian works of literature, there are few descriptions of nature. Yet we need to extend the study to the entire literary output of India to find important passages devoted to this theme. In some epic poems, we find descriptions of oceans, mountains, seasons, forests, night scenes, etc. In this case the contemplation of nature and the attention to emotions that it generates guide the author's selection of images. Here we have direct observation closely tied to the poetic contemplation of nature motifs. This clearly occurs, says Boccali, in the *Rtusambara* (an anonymous work from the fourth century) where, in a passage describing autumn, a dress is compared to grass and a face to the lotus flower; the jangling of the rings on a woman's ankles evokes the call of wild geese and a human torso is like ripe rice in a land bathed in moonlight. In the lyric poem *Meghaduta* (Cloud messenger), also by Kalidasa, a sequence of aerial views in a poetic morphology of mountainous terrain suggests a kind of seeing that translates the object given into an abstract beauty, while at the same time it remains true to perception and the power of the imagination; the result is an image of rivulets that resemble a woman's tresses ("the water is as soft-spun as a hair braid"). Other images of this natural gaze are analyzed, from the standpoint of the rhetorical figures *svabbavokti* (description) and *jati* (description of nature), especially starting with *Kumarasambhava*, also by Kalidasa, where he tells us that the clouds turn red "free of time" as they reflect the colours of the immense caves of red arsenic in the Himalayan mountains. Finally, at the heart of these metaphors per Boccali, we have two strophes from the *Songs of the Monks* from the Buddhist canon, written in Pāli. Here the naturalist poetics outlined above is born. The subject meditates in mountains that go silent, rocks that delight the eyes, and gleaming clouds below which limpid waters flow during the rainy season, while the *kareri*, musky roses of various colours, appear. The physical state of nature extends before the spirit of contemplation as when, according to Boccali, who cites the famous Buddhist poet Ashvaghosha, Siddhartha appears as a radiant point at the top of a mountain, seated in contemplation, as luminous as the moon rising behind thick clouds. And here, echoes of European Romanticism blend with canonical Buddhist elements.

In his various writings on Chinese thought and aesthetics, François Jullien reminds us that the *Dialogues* of Confucius and the works of Mencius and Lao-tzu are not concerned with the general features of essences or categories, but with the integration of the semiotic variants in meaning, underscoring the richness of allusion and implication. In this part of the world, Chuang-tzu, in the third century BCE, also speaks of the importance of wonder in knowledge. Here, too, we have an original model that we could call aesthetic. In his *Book of Nan-hua*, where Taoist culture and Chan Buddhism meet, the author proposes a version of the ultimate philosophy: "How marvellous and how mysterious it is that we do not know where creatures come from! How mysterious and how marvellous it is that at first we cannot even see their images clearly. The ten thousand creatures, in their enormous quantity, all prosper because we do not interfere in their activities" (Chuang-tzu 1998, 91; translated by Corrado Federici).

I will not deal with the alchemical elements in Carl Gustav Jung or the revival of a certain esoteric tradition described by Mircea Eliade, Henry Corbin, and René Guénon, since the topic is too complex to be treated within the thematic framework of the present book. I did reserve a special space for Coomaraswamy, however, because he clarifies the comparative issue as it relates to the Indian perspective. What is worrisome, today, is the fact that the global market is destroying all these points of interaction, in a total cultural and iconographic homologation. Even comparative studies, in this day and age, risk being flattened out, used, and planned in a crude simplified manner.

8 THEORIES OF NON-CONCEPTUALITY

Hans Blumenberg (2010) develops a theory in which he demonstrates that images and metaphors need not be thought of as provisional, incomplete moments in the formation of concepts. Metaphors are part of the structure of the symbolic mind and pertain to the language of the unconscious; they direct the gaze toward the present but point to what is absent; they narrate what is seen as well as what is not. Metaphors come into existence when words in a given context are configured in such a way that they mean something other than what they denote. In this conscious and unconscious interplay between reality and illusion, we detach ourselves from the object and make present what is absent, thereby creating a new act of contemplation and perception, because implied in this process is a return to the object now enriched by a new, impalpable but necessary sensibility. By uniting separate and different elements, the image becomes accessible as it presides over the unexpected. It is a way of detaching oneself, or pretending to detach oneself, in order to return to the thing. Metaphors are an aesthetic medium. Thus, with our imagination, we traverse a kingdom of symbols that represent what is before our eyes. When we observe and contemplate a city, we can read it as if it were a book; it seems to have a language endowed with a rhetorical code, albeit a precarious one, related to the volatility of feelings, but still a "language" of objects and relationships.

In the mid-1970s, Paul Ricoeur discussed the many modes of discourse and sought to describe the core meaning of metaphor by relating it to the languages of re-description and to the metamorphosis of reality. In light of these arguments, wherein we abandon our habitual relationships with language, as well as Blumenberg's more recent observations cited in the preceding paragraph, we are in a position to deal with the "rhetoric" of architecture and of the structure of the city, which are both material and non-material or symbolic expressions of the places of the community. In this way we can grasp new dimensions of the things that appear before us as well as the changes in meaning associated with them, which result from the intentionality of the visitor-viewer, the architect, the writer, or reader writ large.

In "Architecture and Narrativity" (2016), Ricoeur takes up Mikhail Bakhtin's notion of the chronotope, or the fusion of the spatial and temporal references in a novel, involving the cultural interconnection of subject and object. He identifies the "act of inhabiting" and the "act of building" that constitute narratives in terms of elements of internal and external space that become interrelated or inscribed into one another. By examining the temporal aspects of the inhabiting-building acts, he arrives at a complete rethinking of the exchange dynamic between the spatiality of the narrative and the temporality of the architectural project. Ricoeur uses three terms: "prefiguration," "configuration," and "refiguration." Places, or points where something happens, become part of the storyline. But the act of narrating can be distinguished from imitative action (mimesis), thereby revealing a narrative intelligibility that makes possible the interpretation of the built space as a reflective and rationalizing activity. Here, Ricoeur refers to Aristotelian *mythos* and poiesis that produce stories, but he does so to reaffirm the involvement of the reader who, in this process of rationalization of the discourse, seems to have been abandoned. Structuralism, then, is made to meet hermeneutics; in architectural *making*, the primary act of configuration, i.e., the "temporal synthesis of the heterogeneous" in narrative, corresponds to the "spatial synthesis of the heterogeneous" (2016, 36). We note that the materials of the building have variables that are relatively independent of each other: units of space, forms, and boundary surfaces. The architectural project tends to create objects in which various aspects come together to form a certain unity and the building becomes, before our eyes, a polyphonic message to be read simultaneously as encompassing and analytical. In the configuration phase, there is a time of building and a time of built space, a condensed time. Now the creative gaze opens up a mobile space that runs through the structure, and descriptive intelligence is invested by the mobility of the gaze in its historicity, of which it leaves traces or marks: something always precedes the writer as something always precedes the architect. In this phase there is a tendency to celebrate language as such; architecture aims at being "pure" architecture; from the standpoint of literature, this coincided with the turning point represented by Alain Robbe-Grillet and Marguerite Duras, a language in which words detach themselves from things, either in a spirit of abstraction or a spirit of radical naturalism. This is the moment of refiguration where the exchange of meanings creates new possibilities for inhabiting and narrating the world in a transformative way, one that aims at intertextuality and the opening up of possibilities. Summing up, in the prefiguration phase the acts of inhabiting and building were practically the same thing; in the configuration phase the built space or architectural project prevails; and in the refiguration phase the inhabiting reacts to the building and proposes a reading of expectations, becomes plural and intertextual. Only in this way is the city an amalgam of narrated time and built space, because from this emerges the world of the text, the lived world of revelation and transformation. On the level of refiguration, narrative and architecture avail themselves of a double articulation: a spatial-temporal world based on the relationship between universal time and historical time mediated by the places of memory, and a spatial-temporal world based on the relationship between geometric space and inhabited space mediated by the histories inscribed in these places of memory. Finally, what is the spatial interlocutor of the narrative identity? Ricoeur's answer is *itinérance* (itinerancy) or the movement of the flâneur, which lies midway between wandering and the feeling of the domestic or the familiar; it is an adaptation of Bakhtin's chronotope: a space that becomes a world full of the most consonant possibilities. Happy is the architect, he says, that "plans new ways to inhabit, which will be inserted in the tangle of these already past life stories" (37).

Buildings and cities that narrate and novels that build explain the aesthetic meaning of the principle of narration in architecture and in literature: a composite identity of materials and forms, of things and metaphors, and of the material and the non-material capable of establishing and motivating, in the intermediate act of spatializing time and temporalizing space, the evocative myth of the word and the deployment of building techniques. This is not Daniel Libeskind's ethical approach, and it does not suggest the imaginary of a J.R.R. Tolkien or a H.P. Lovecraft. We can find examples of this narrativity in the works of architects like Emilio Ambasz, Renzo Piano, and Frank Gehry, as well as in the literary works of Italo Calvino, James Ballard, and Don DeLillo. Such architects and writers have applied, either consciously or unconsciously and in an exemplary fashion, the poietic wandering through the structures and images of a vision that essentially connotes the intimate communication between architecture and literature through the techniques of narration.

The correlation between literature and architecture could be extended to music as suggested by Friedrich T. Vischer who, in his *Aesthetics*, advocates the importance of the musical gesture. We have already mentioned the gesture as a constitutive part of creativity. Vischer claims that music is the gestural acoustic language of feeling, and that the gesture is nothing other than a symbolism of spiritual acts. This is an interesting observation in the light of the anamnesis that we can now transfer from the visible and the verbal to the aural. Important to note here is the fact that the flow of sounds is somewhat analogous to the state of mind in representation, and that the former brings to mind the latter. The theme of memory and reminiscence, in both the clinical and the Platonic sense, reappears in music: the *mythopoiea* of forms and figures returns in this case and clarifies how music is represented and how music represents itself, through the gesture, and with a rhythmical "spasm." For Vischer, music is essentially not so much an adequate expression of the state of mind as an analogy. The musical gesture is, in fact, a thread that connects the arts, not a state of mind.

Now an observation on the difference between associative representation and empathy: association and representation go together; the former is secondary in relation to objects, while the latter is connected to them; associative representation brings something else along with it and displays it, like an image, including by means of incidental memories, but it is not really empathy. It is connected to it in certain cases because empathy is self-activating; think of colour and its internal or symbolic representations. The pleasure of pure forms operates between mathematical-geometric pleasure and the tactile element in empathy. Harmony, which is the expression of empathy, is accompanied by the act of perceiving in a mimesis of life and becomes a symbolic presence. The beautiful unites harmony and mimesis in a flowering of schemas where image and meaning are stimulated by an act or a gesture that moves both image and meaning to create seductive personifications. The importance of the gesture and the act, even in representation as outlined earlier, works on and in contemplation. Nothing is the object of contemplation if it is not internally perceived in a synthetic way relative to the multiplicity of the event, the given, or the object that becomes personal in a process wherein elements gradually become unified and coordinated. I am present in my inner motion and activity, per Antonio Prete. In contemplation I am inside the object that I look at. Every line or figure changes in me as I contemplate and live in its forms while following its contours, components, extensions, and modifications. When we contemplate forms, we experience activities as something firmly connected to forms. This applies to art, but it also applies to nature. Each time I meditate on nature, I belong to it by virtue of my inner activity, my waiting, acting, and bringing something to completion. The objects of nature, like those of art, are humanized. Theodor Lipps expresses the following thought in this regard: "Aesthetic contemplation is a contemplation whose only interest is the contemplation and enjoyment of the aesthetic object. For those who contemplate aesthetically, the object always constitutes a world in itself, one that is absolutely beyond any real world. We can define this being beyond all real worlds as an aesthetic ideal of the aesthetic object" (1997, 196; translated by Corrado Federici).

But we need to be careful because this act is associated with the fact that I myself experience the contemplation of the object; there is no separation but rather empathy. With respect to this interpretation of contemplation as it relates to empathy, Lipps goes on the explain the psychological state of the self and of consciousness: "In contemplating the massive crag, I enjoy the same power within me, except that I enjoy it like an empathized power. I enjoy the powerful inner tension that the nature of the crag stirs within me ... absorbed in its contemplation" (1997, 198).

9 ON BEING A GAZE

There is a daemon in nature that affects us on both the intimate and the historical level; it appears in the context of symbolic forms. In the 1930s Mario Untersteiner ([1938] 2019) explained that in Homer the daemon is described as a spiritual force of the divine, both visible and invisible, and present on the earth. It is on this basis that we can begin to analyze the gaze, our gaze, and its role in the "knowledge of the senses."

We are discussing nature and its forms within the frame of the principal aesthetic categories developed from the seventeenth century including the age of Goethe, up to the twentieth. What opens up in front of us, then, is a complex series of reflections on nature that look back to Renaissance-era and, further, Greco-Roman thought, while casting a disconsolate glance forward to the present age. As we know, these reflections had a specific theme and terminology articulated in theories propounded from Romanticism to the poetics of the twentieth century. I am particularly interested in this cluster of topics and problems as they appear in the postmodern aesthetics of fragmentation, pastiche, relativism, and the like, convinced, that nature and art constitute a unique, indivisible heritage to be preserved and re-proposed.

To this end, what is required is an ethics of idea and behaviour that promotes a humanization of forms in cities especially, in terms of reviving the creation and design of vegetable and flower gardens, hedges and terraces, and green walls of vegetation. This should be done so that the culture of doing does not generate, as is often the case in recent epochs, two distinct and discordant visions of the poiesis of the communities: the widespread use of asphalt and cement in urban areas, on the one hand, and the establishment of protected areas, with the resulting confusion as regards public policy in our historical context.

In this regard, philosophical ideas on nature and the landscape, or the most recent technological innovations, are not overlooked. From the study of aesthetic and artistic categories from the Enlightenment to Romanticism (the sublime, picturesque, neo-gothic, romantic, and then symbolic), there emerge different views of the world as thought, imagined, and described, at times with nostalgia, by philosophers, scientists, artists, and writers. This collection presents nature as an absolute, on the one hand, and the landscape as a reality and as representation of human work, on the other.

All this is still perceptible in the culture of "landscapists," from futurist to deconstructive; it is congenial to their spirit of description and planning: an architectural, agronomic, and humanistic vocation.

What is important to note here is something ancient, both particular and universal, simple and tangible, the thing that draws or foregrounds our attention as landscapists when we are a gaze; in other words, when sensibility and mind combine to create the bases for chance occurrences and relationships, for memory and matter. This is the way I would like to describe an aesthetic gaze, whether in performance or in contemplation that awaits, per William Wordsworth's *The Prelude*, in a "holy calm," within us, dream-like images (2:371–5). Through such mental immersion, we understand what a landscape is: nature simultaneously an image of essence and the resonance it creates within us.

This can be explained in the light of a dynamics of feeling. The gaze moves among visible features, unites and divides elements and shapes, takes in the panorama, then loses itself in the space among vegetation and mineral formations. Whether motionless or in motion, the gaze wanders as it searches for meaning in forms that change and imaginative metaphors that reconfigure those forms. It is a gaze that sees, scrutinizes, retains, and contemplates in order to wander about itself in a web of perceptions and imaginings. It delights in moving among the signs of arboreal life and those of human life. Recognizing, investigating, admiring, and capturing the fragility and the design of everything that surrounds us is a pleasant mental adventure nourished by the varieties of beauty that arise out of the void existing between things. The senses and the heart adjust as the joy of participation permeates them, thereby creating the sensation of floating on the ether suspended over places observed. By abandoning the quotidian scene of shock and provocation, we situate the sign of the object between reality and representation. Those who stroll live concretely in the intermediate space, in the regions of the mind, sight, and feeling, in such a way as to make mind, sight, and feeling their own without depleting them. Those who love the landscape seek out silence in order to tend to the landscape. Even if they were to enter physically degraded places, they would attempt mentally to reconstruct them as images of serenity suitable for a new haven. At that particular moment, their suspended gaze becomes a refuge; only nature seems to speak to them in its mute language, its own alphabet, as piercing and rustling sounds emerge, sometimes gradually and other times suddenly. We appreciate silence precisely because it allows itself to be perceived between the empty spaces between sounds, like colours and symbols on a white sheet. Before a nature that "loves to hide," according to Heraclitus, silence prospers in freedom, not constrained in waiting; rather, it is the waiting of the word itself. We are a gaze; and so a landscapist tends to the present and the past, what is and what could be. Silence is the soul of perception that proceeds to feeling; it nudges us toward pensiveness and concentration in order to enable vision to attain its best results; hence, the landscapist becomes an interpreter, narrator, and planner.

The computer lends itself to exploratory, affective, and even combinatorial creativity but much less so to transformational creativity, which constructs representational and poietic paradigms of the human mind, according to Marcus du Sautoy (2019). It functions best in the visual arts in developing this kind of representation. With machines, it is difficult to reproduce transformational creativity, linguistic paradigms, and symbolic universes, and to invent philosophy, music, literature, and the planning that presupposes social, anthropological intelligence, so that there is a rapport between, on the one hand, the bodily energies of emotions, passions, and fears (which constitute the supporting structure of the human brain that creates social integration), and, on the other hand, the sensory stimulation caused by sights, smells, sounds and the like. Machines try to reproduce all this but, apart from the impossibility of such, there is the potential danger of their misuse by individuals or groups who want to control people.

Machines Like Me, a novel by Ian McEwen already mentioned and which deals with the theme of next-generation robots and the coexistence of machines and humans, recreates the atmosphere of Steven Spielberg's film *A.I. Artificial Intelligence* (2001). In both novel and film, the power of attraction concerns the mind as well as the affective habits.

10 THE ART OF SEEING AND FEELING

We need to experience the state of grace that is silence by disconnecting ourselves from ordinary life and stopping, so we can breathe and contemplate for a moment the rarefied and vivid aura of the elements of the cosmos (air, water, earth, fire). The imagination sustains, piques, and enlivens interest and curiosity in a free play of images. The ecstatic moment is itself a pensive one, but it suddenly tends to permeate everything. Silence is nourished by such moments when we observe and admire the astounding variety of things, when, in a certain light, the sight of a forest, field, tree, or flower can become a refuge. This is the point at which, sensing the unsayable and the inexpressible aspect of the view, consciousness, no longer mute and absorbed in expectation of the word, dissolves. In this state silence creates images in which we immerse ourselves with wonder. The contemplative state is a "state of reception" that originates in the fact that the ecstatic mind promotes the birth of a new "thought" capable of neutralizing the unidirectional flow of consciousness. What counts here is the suspension of time, a special time for listening, in other words, a time of silence. To listen from the perspective of silence, in fact, implies seeing differently. In this way silence and solitude allow us to become reacquainted with the perception of our inner selves and the world around us. Whereas in ordinary experience the external world fills the inner world, now the exterior and interior dimensions interact in correspondence to each other.

The gaze is our guide in this process. The solitary stroller realizes that he or she is the protagonist of an absolute vision. This is what happens in Rousseau's Seventh Walk, when the solitary walker reveals to the reader a spirit that grows more responsive as it surrenders to the ecstasy that harmony stirs in him. The senses dissolve in a sweet and profound reverie, and he is lost in a delightful intoxication in the immensity in which he feels immersed. And so, individual objects elude him; he sees and feels nothing but the whole of nature, Rousseau says. Vision and feeling move together through a conjunction of aesthetic beauty and emotions, in a recomposed mosaic of dispersed identities where elements become performers in a cosmic dance. As our gaze proceeds, stone, water, and sand come apart and dissolve in a froth of energy, a colour dust cloud. We feel ourselves being swept into the world itself, before the descriptive and creative processes of pictorial, literary, and architectural representation are activated. Sensation is emotional and representation is mental. As pure and simple as trees, flowers, valleys, mountains, fields, and sky, everything in nature seems to approach us, becomes graspable and experienced in the grace of our extraordinary state. The perceptible becomes presence that gradually becomes imperceptible and silent. In this condition seeing overlays imagining and dreaming. Once we go beyond observing, beyond the details of a minute description, we withdraw into a totally private and untouchable meditation, in a gaze that surpasses seeing itself. We translate the act of seeing into a ritual of time and space, as we commingle the senses and the mind in order to concentrate on the image we want to preserve and we consider to be absolutely ours. To contemplate means to attribute to nature, whether the spontaneous one or the one produced by human work, an eminently aesthetic value. We feel that the gaze is alive; it "breathes" in the aura of the vast mountain terrain or the joy of a tree branch that shades us from the sun and that, moved by a breeze, seems to touch the sky.

One who contemplates, disregarding space and time, and objectivity and subjectivity, tends to lose herself in a transcending of forms: that person becomes a protagonist that replaces the figures in the cosmos of the representational arts. Everything hovers, then, in a continuous interplay of impressions, sensations, and images: a flower, shrub, tree, clearing in the woods, field, crag, or stream can become a sanctuary against the violence of the contemporary world, which seems a factory for producing endless conflicts and objects that are all the same. It is an occasion for re-establishing an *originary* connection, one rich in myths and symbols, and we seek it out precisely in silence in order to fashion the art of an initial representation. The encounter with the daemon of living forms suggests a secret understanding that can assuage the pains of a mundane existence. The daemon who wanders among landscapes and among visitors strews sacred phantasms all around, separating the sacred from the profane. Consciousness enters into this borderland between the human and the divine in an extraordinary encounter with God (for Christians) or with the abyssal mystery of nature (for others). We are always surprised by wonder when, absorbed in seeing, our minds are emptied of thoughts and filled with beauty, in a silence wherein we feel that we are the sunlight, the air current, the rolling sea, and the shimmering stars. Silence is the vehicle we use to see and do.

We are discussing contemplation here. Aristotle (*Nicomachean Ethics*, 1177a–b) places at the base of Western thought precisely the contemplative life, which he considers to be the highest or perfect virtue, and a life lived in conformity with virtue is a happy life. This activity, the most divine part of us, is to be thought of as a continuous theoretical "pleasure" that coincides with wisdom. The wise and contemplative individual is entirely self-sufficient and possesses all the qualities; his lifestyle, which deviates from the practices of politics and war, and operates with dignity and without goals, is the happiest of all because it transcends human nature. There is something of the divine in such blessed individuals; in fact, to the extent possible, they tend to make themselves immortal by living in accordance with the noblest part of themselves. What is more, contemplation is cherished for its own sake; nothing comes from it except the act of having contemplated, unlike other practical virtues from which we derive some good. Aristotle's words are at the core of quiet meditation in subsequent centuries, as we find in Seneca's *Moral Letters to Lucilius* (6, 56) and in the unfolding of Christianity. Contemplation is also a fundamental part of our appreciation of what I have referred to as landscapes of silence; it does not correspond to the Kantian sublime and the pleasure we get from fear, nor aesthetic dismay, nor "pleasurable agitation" at the sight of volcanic eruptions and storms. In the contemplative state, we do not find the cacophony of extreme life but a calming confluence of images.

II DIALOGUES ON NATURE

Solitary contemplators, these new *amateurs* of nature escape anguish and roam the vast territorial habitats that are the contemporary megacities with a new peregrine spirit and no specific destination in mind. Like modern-day monks, they advocate a return to the land and breathe in the spirit of anti-consumerism. Only distance creates the right relationship between the subject and the world as it appears and as it is represented. Like Ralph Waldo Emerson and Henry David Thoreau, along with their predecessors from antiquity, they make our hearts beat in tune with that of nature in a harmony of souls strolling among living forms. Objects and ornaments merge with forms in a subtle sensibility. Everything is suspended when we abandon the harsher aspects of existence and history. The gaze loves to irradiate. The landscape of silence invites us to encounter a manifestation of the divine, where we can situate ourselves, our dreams, and our representations. In this way we manage to touch the essence of the activity of seeing. Those who contemplate the landscape for the purpose of enjoying the splendour of nature and an intimate relationship with it escape fear, such as the dread they experience before the apocalyptic image of entire territories shrouded in smog or callously poisoned by heaps of garbage. In this sense the landscape of silence is a gift, but it is an achievement as well. It comes to us unexpectedly, on the heels of patient waiting. An enigma with transitions and transformations that the narrative spirit leads back to poetic truth assumes concrete form next to us in a sort of drama of metamorphoses: a flow of forms inscribed by the rhythm of the life of the universe and the symbols of its secret language. This healing gaze is also hope.

Throughout human history we have often wondered what the disasters that repeatedly shake the sense of security of the human species as it evolves mean. Unexpectedly, cyclically, or randomly, what has been built up with labour and the application of technical skill is undone, destroyed, or erased. Whether the damage is caused by external agents or by humanity itself, a tragic destiny has always accompanied us, and each time we are overwhelmed, we rebuild. Each time misfortune gets us in its inexorable grip, the collective mind sets itself to work among the ruins and mourning, visualizing its resurgence by drawing up a plan, design, or project. Despite everything, we are nature within nature, and this relationship cannot be undone. In whatever way we make art, we naturalize it, and, conversely, in whatever way we ourselves are naturalized, we make art. Every act involves a doing that is conditioned by imagining, thinking, and planning a "rehabilitative" schema with respect to an object dear to us that has been destroyed. We need to intervene in a continuous manner, and there is no poiesis without phantasia. We are defined by symbolic thought and the spirit of wandering in the practice of sensory experimentation. But how is this done? Opinions with respect to judgment, recognition, and identity can be expressed in varying degrees. This *how* is the most fragile and obscure point, because the idea, tied to the act of making something appear, should entail an appropriate and corresponding ethics, a responsible behaviour that takes care of what once existed and thus of memory. At the same time, the idea preserves the place as it was and thus the forms that are repositories of the life lived by its inhabitants. Culture and knowledge, both traditional and new techniques, form a network of potential relationships. I would argue that an ontology of misfortunes is reflected in an ontology of representation in an effort to suggest a scenario of hope to set against the tragic course of civilization. In the face of terrible, incomprehensible, and uncontrollable forces, examples of material intervention alternate with the physiologies of the emotions. In this middle zone, architecture puts on display all of its genius, as it runs the great risk of producing projects that inevitably bring it into contact with the political sphere.

"What it is like, what it was like, what it will be like": this is the theatre of the gaze and feeling, of ascertainment and perspective, as well as of exploration and distance. It is also the space for describing and narrating to others in order to offer them an image that they can no longer possess. As Marc Augé claims, "For there to be a landscape, we need not only a gaze but also a conscious perception, a judgment, and a description. The landscape is the space described by one person to another person" (2004, 72; translated by Corrado Federici).

As has been argued, we cannot detach ourselves from the gaze because every landscape exists only for the gaze that discovers it. It presupposes at least a witness, an observer. "All landscapes that seem most natural to us owe something to the work of humans, and those that seem to be totally autonomous have been at least accessed by a network of communication routes and technical devices that allow us to make use of them as landscapes" (Augé 2004, 72).

This quote can strike us as a statement of fact or it can suggest a poetic, indirect, or metaphoric evocation. The power of words is necessary when someone who has seen speaks to someone who has not seen. In this the imagination of others is stimulated.

We can say that, when confronted with disasters, human beings try to organize or reorganize what they consider to be important and common procedures required for a concrete resolution of the problem. They try to realize, through plans and principles, various ideas that they consider to be of absolute priority, categories that seem to be perennial.

In the Western tradition, the concept of *disegno*, in the sense of physical drawing and creative design, is considered to be the father of the arts of painting, sculpture, and architecture. This is true for Giorgio Vasari, Leonardo, Raphael, and Michelangelo. Disegno is a founding idea, an essence that structures representation; it pertains both to human images and to things; it encompasses all of nature. Erwin Panofsky has dealt skilfully with disegno in this sense. For him, it encompasses experience and emotions in a grand orchestration of signs: it illustrates, describes, projects, and visualizes the entire world. The city is also, essentially, a design, the product of a vision and imitation, the work of forms and traces, an image of masses and surfaces, the art of planning and technology, a creative whole or a wondrous poiesis that can be enclosed within a schema that is at once practical and ideal. All the random doing and building that humankind has been able to produce over three millennia was given order or organized structure. From the ancient Greek and Roman model to those of the Renaissance up to the nineteenth century, the city is the result of a design. For more than a century, however, disegno has been devalued; the idea has lost its centre, and civilization is undergoing a crisis of symbolic function. And this is occurring precisely at a time when the city's strongest presence in terms of design is being expressed. The structure that held the city, landscape, things, and events together in a single idea, however composite it may have been, has split apart: practices, techniques, languages, and customs have undone the ensemble that is now sprouting into a thousand branches, emptying itself of meaning and throwing out new, improvised, anonymous, and disorganized offshoots.

12 SOCIAL AND POLITICAL REPRESENTATION

When we speak of representation, we cannot help but also think of the system of political proxies that historically drive the collective consciousness to create connections and networks of social relations. So much so in that representation produces an actual "social art" founded on perception and communication. Essentially, this social art is the product of a development the aim of which is a positive outcome for everyone, namely, the creation of a common spirit and mentality. According to Niklas Luhmann's *Art as a Social System* (2000), this feature is based on aspects of closed and open structures (self-referential and hetero-referential) as can be found in conscious and unconscious nervous systems. Even the images of this social dimension, from the time of medieval wall or floor mosaics to the present, weave together forms of representation and shared experience whose organization holds together what must not be broken down. Those who contemplate and those who admire participate in such an experience and become a single entity. This situation is multiplied through the many mass media effects and tools.

Building also on Talcott Parsons's analysis of structural variables (*The System of Modern Societies*, 1971) and Eric Voegelin's study of the nature of symbolic representation (*Order and History*, 1956–87), the theory of social systems investigates the historical roots of violence and evil in human actions, where the emphasis on what is contemplated is much greater than on the ethical consequences of contemplation. The theme of the communicative fascination with cruel acts, the function of mass stereotypes, the justification of ideological crimes, and the seductive power of evil witnessed in the last century, with profound ramifications for the present, attracts scholarly attention, most notably on the part of Salvatore Natoli (2019) and Oriana Binik (2019). Contemplation of the object becomes an ecstatic exaltation of the power of the represented object; the individual who contemplates departs from the scene and is replaced by his walk-on. Pier Paolo Portinaro (2017) is perhaps most relevant on this score, as he points to a person's capacity to process sense impressions and ideas or, crucially, the impact of something unexpected that has the capacity to move us, in the obscurity of our feelings, to savour the intoxicating feeling of self-assuredness as we absolve ourselves of the most frightening crimes. Genocide and, from the early twentieth century onward, democide are events that recur in our history: a long list of massacres, episodes of ethnic cleansing, and mass executions. The execution of minorities (a small part of the demos) has been carried out in the Soviet Union, China, North Korea, and Cambodia. (The killing of the majority of the demos is essentially impossible because the extermination of the workforce necessary for the survival of any modern society must be avoided.)

This problem lies at the root of the representation of who we are. According to Sigmund Freud, a self-destructive impulse is the source of violence. And the observation most pertinent for us is the following: "The dark sense of guilt that has hung over humanity since primitive times, and which in some religions has condensed in the hypothesis of an original sin, is probably the manifestation of a blood-guilt with which primitive man had burdened himself" (2014, aphorism no. 9).

Accompanying this image is that of the scapegoat or the search for one's own invulnerability in the face of the extraordinary and the excess of "circumstances" discussed by Elias Canetti in *Massa e potere* (Crowds and power, 1981). Working our way back through the millennia, we find the *originary* paradigm of ethno-religious crime in the political actions of great ancient empires, as in those of the Assyrians and perhaps Egyptians – these being among the earliest. The image of slaughters and deportations are ever present: the leitmotif of history and myth is extermination, deportation, and enslavement.

All this weighs on the personal and collective unconscious with seductions that may be not only calculated but also unforeseeable or impromptu. We depict and personify power; we see and represent ourselves in a world of appearances and social forms that we recognize and that satisfy, or should satisfy, our sense of belonging to a thriving community. Everything flows from an initial narrative of living together, a myth that was also perverted by Freud's understanding of the primitive sense of guilt. As Giuseppe Duso (2016) tells us, political representation contains a perennial problem related to the seduction of power: the image we have of representation is an effective symbol in that it is not disconnected from reality, as we can clearly see from

Plato's *Republic* as regards the polis. Since ancient times, reflection on representation cannot help implying an ontology of the image. We, in fact, find ourselves confronted with a series of interactions based on conflicts between the image of what is represented and the impact of the spectator on the image. The addressee of the representation changes, or can change, the image. With Gadamer's *Truth and Method* (2000) in mind, Duso (2016) notes the double nature of this structure of representation. In fact, on the basis of the stereotype of the image of the ruler, we can say that even in the present era of mass media authority represents itself precisely by making itself an image in the eyes of its subjects. The fact that this is a public event is an integral part of representation: the image acquires its "authenticity" precisely because the ruler must be represented. By presenting himself to the public, the ruler no longer belongs to himself, in the sense that he must be like the image wants him to be. The virtuality of today's mass media technology confirms even more extensively and systematically this dialectic of the image and representation in a cultural setting. There is an image (*eikon*) that is faithful to its nature as image, which points to the object of which it is the image, and there is an image (*phantasma*), which betrays its direct representation by concealing its relationship with the object of which it is the image and by presenting itself as autonomous. This symbolic slippage and doubling influences human actions, causes the appearance of the model of the idea (or form) to develop socially and concretely in terms of the movement of the will that presumes to be a true interpretation and a representation of objects. From this existential situation, we can also identify political form as a symbolic representational image operative in mass psychology. This, however, is an additional theme that enables us to understand the vastness of the society of the spectacle (Debord 1967).

3

Harmony

Harmony condenses within itself the meanings of active and passive contemplation and distributes them along a continuum that includes art, nature, and culture. It places the beauty of the arts and aesthetic life at the centre of its vortex of sensibility and forms, reconciles differences and contrasts, heals the wounded gaze, makes the extraordinary very familiar to everyone, turns the chaos of sounds and motions into music, and tends to bring happiness to relations and practices. Harmony is a process of composing and recomposing that slowly weaves a whole philosophy of representations that unites reason with feeling. Amid the effects of artificial reality, in the confusion in today's world, it weaves the threads of tradition into worldviews as it traverses the pathways of imitation in the places of myth and history, enlivening the effects of the synesthetic metaphor and providing a gaze that evokes nature and culture through time.

Harmony is an art of contemplation, an enlightened technique capable of aesthetically shaping human destiny through emotions and forms of knowledge. It dreams of antiquity as the future while it revises models that seem to be eternal; it rides on the wings of the symbol and traces graceful auras in the atlas of historical-stylistic categories. In art treatises it prefigures consonances and proportions in the idea of the divine and the natural order. Leonardo, Michelangelo, Raphael, and Gian Lorenzo Bernini came to understand the harmony of the body through music. In addition, within the system of art, harmony revivifies the canon by rejecting the tendency to reduce aesthetics to ideology and by adapting the absolute to solitude, which is the noblest form of our confrontation with the mortal world. Just as we can think of poetry in terms of perfection as a dynamic process, the same can be said for painting, music, and the other arts.

2 ORDER

By harmony, speaking figuratively, we normally mean a correspondence between feeling and thought that creates a general sense of peace and serenity. This idea originates in aesthetics where it expresses a complex correlation between perceptual signs and objective givens, a "coexistence of parts" or concord of tones. As Goethe writes to Karl Ludwig von Knebel (17 November 1789), "Thus is every creature but one tone, one hue of a great harmony which one must study in whole and at large, lest every particular become a dead letter" (quoted in Richards 2002, 175). With this felicitous integration of the particular and the universal, the poet clarifies in a pithy statement a meaning of the term that, as quoted, is tied to the concept of tonality. This tonality we can call affective or specific to the mental categories in which concepts fuse together with sensory impressions and feelings. Harmony is a fundamental notion in thought and in art, a philosophical tool and a manifestation of the aesthetic life. It exists in the space between reality and judgment, and it is capable of providing a vast field of knowledge in theory and experience. As an aesthetic category, harmony also reflects the constant change in the status of forms and becomes the measure of the relationships in our judgments as regards sensibility, techniques, and creative processes.

In music, harmony is the consonance of voices or instruments, a combination of chords, i.e., simultaneous sounds, as well as an association of successive sounds capable of producing an impression that is pleasant to the ear and the spirit. As we know, it is also the science of chord construction. On first reading, it represents the "vertical," as opposed to the "horizontal," aspect of the melodic line. In reality music is neither vertical nor horizontal, and we cannot consider only the harmonic or contrapuntal aspect of a musical composition. Yet it is necessary to think of a certain feature of music as vertical in theory and teaching in order to establish a nomenclature for the basic chords and to justify their categorization in consonant and dissonant chords. It may also be useful for systematizing the general rules of the concatenation of chords on which modulation and the cadenza in particular rely. Shifting our attention to the other arts, we observe that in literature harmony is associated with analogy and onomatopoeia (examples of so-called imitative harmony), which produce an evocative phonic effect. Harmony originates in a "musical" juxtaposition of accents and pauses, in the arrangement of the words and phrases that renders the discourse pleasurable within an organized whole. In architecture, painting, and the plastic arts in general, harmony is the order of the parts relative to the whole, held together by accord, proportion, and the proper arrangement of elements.

3 MEASURE

The concept of harmony was originally formulated in the school of Pythagoras in whose cosmology we find speculation on music. The Pythagoreans succeeded in identifying the seven notes, describing the octave as "harmony." The basic notes of this scale, from which the other notes are derived, are the first, fourth or *diatesseron*, and fifth or *diapente*, the octave, as well as the four notes of Philolaus's tetrachord (do, fa, sol, do). Through observation and experimentation, Pythagoras discovered that the relationships between the length of the strings and notes was expressed in numerical ratios of 4:3, 3:2, 2:1, that is to say, by the relationships among the numbers of the *tetractys* (the number 10, the sum of the first four numbers, which can be represented by an equilateral triangle consisting of four rows: 1, 2, 3, and 4 points). Philolaus demonstrated that harmony is based on the same four numbers (1, 2, 3, 4) found in the tetractys. On the subject of harmony, we need to point out as well that the sect of Acousmatics, linked to the oldest and most uncorrupted Pythagorean tradition, claimed its seat in the sanctuary of Apollo in Delphi. This observation opens up a whole symbolic and metaphorical field because harmony, considered contained within the tetractys, is seen as containing the Sirens, who represent the harmony of the spheres and are connected to the sacred function of music in Pythagoreanism. We read the following passage from Plato's *Republic*, which comes after the description of the eight whorls: "And the spindle turned on the knees of Necessity, and up above on each of the rims of the circles a Siren stood, borne around in its revolution and uttering one sound, one note, and from all the eight there was the concord of a single harmony" (617b–c).

Each on a throne, three other women sat in a circle at an equal distance from the others. They were the sisters of Ananke, the Fates, dressed in white robes and wearing wreaths on their heads: Lachesis, Clotho, and Atropos. They sang in harmony with the Sirens: Lachesis sang the past, Clotho the present, and Atropos the future. At intervals, Clotho moved the outer circle with her right hand, Atropos grasped the inner circle with her left, and Lachesis moved now one and now the other with both hands. This is an image that, by analogy, relates to the creation myth and the birth of the world out of pure sound. We see reflected here the symbolism of the Pythagoreans, who saw the cosmos as ordered in accordance with the simple numerical relationships of the realm of sound, and so the spheres of the planets in their reciprocal distances corresponded to the musical intervals. In the popular version, this doctrine taught that the true notes in precise relationships to each other were ejected by the motion of the celestial bodies, their great velocity and diameter of their orbits. The passage from Plato cited above leads us into an extensive area of analogical thinking whose truth lies in mythology as natural philosophy in disguise conveyed by a poetic image.

4 CORRESPONDENCES

There exist at least three meanings of "harmony." The first takes us back to Pythagoras and resurfaces for the most part in the classical and medieval periods. It refers to the segmentation of a vibrating string, in accordance with precise arithmetical ratios that produce euphonic sounds that relate to the sound produced by the whole vibrating string. As noted above, this basic physical law is projected onto the cosmological scale and, as a result, harmony is understood as the relationship between what exists on earth and what exists in the celestial spheres. Hence, the "music of the spheres" can be taken literally, and harmony can be understood as the relationship between the spheres and the earth. Extended to the work of art, harmony ensures the canonical cosmological relations. A harmonious statue does not reflect the real forms of the body but rather its ideal forms relative to purely intelligible ones that remain hidden. The main advocate of this point of view is Plotinus. Treatise 6 of book 1 of the *Enneads* contains all the essential elements of metaphysical harmony that would later be highlighted in the domain of aesthetics. Plotinus bases his definition of beauty on similarity and communion with the One. In the paragraph titled "On dialectic [The upward way]," we read that the music lover "must learn to distinguish the material forms from the Authentic-Existent which is the source of all these correspondences and out of the entire reasoned scheme in the work of art: he must be led to the Beauty that manifests itself through these forms; he must be shown that what ravished him was none other than the Harmony of the Intellectual world" (1, 3).

What is pursued, then, is the beauty of intelligible harmony rather than a specific form or manifestation of beauty. Furthermore, the music lover uses philosophical arguments to uphold his belief in realities that "he possessed unconsciously." Elsewhere, Plotinus speaks of imperceptible and perceptible harmonies. The latter are produced by imperceptible harmonies. The senses reveal the imperceptible harmonies to the soul, which is able to intuit their beauty in that these harmonies disclose the identical in the different. Perceptible harmonies are "not arbitrary but are determined by the Principle whose labour is to dominate Matter and bring pattern into being" (1, 6). In other words, "beauties of the realm of sense ... have entered into Matter to adorn and to ravish, where they are seen" (1, 6).

In classical antiquity and in the Middle Ages, a harmonious relation and the beauty that it creates are objective facts. The harmony of the cosmos is reflected in objects. The definition of beauty contained in Thomas Aquinas's *Summa theologiae* (Summary of theology) encapsulates this idea. Beauty includes three conditions: *integritas* (wholeness), since things that are not whole are ugly for the same reason; *consonantia* (proportionality); and *claritas* (radiance), from which derive what are called beautiful things that are clear.

The second meaning of harmony shifts our attention from the cosmological level of entities to the psychological level of the spectator. In sixteenth- and seventeenth-century aesthetics, during empiricism's heyday, harmony is, especially with Lord Shaftesbury and Francis Hutcheson, included within theories of sensibility. Beauty, and along with it harmony, are primarily sensations experienced uniquely by the subject who seeks "uniformity in variety."

In a third meaning, harmony is the interplay of faculties. Kant bases the universality of aesthetic judgments not on cosmic harmony but on a common functioning of the faculties involved in making judgments. This subjective judgment of the object, or the representation we have of it, precedes the pleasure of the object itself. In this sense harmony is unequivocally not a harmony of the parts of the object. It exists within the human faculties and the transcendent way in which they operate.

Harmony suffers the same fate as beauty, with which it is intimately connected. Both tend to fade in the modern aesthetic vocabulary because they imply an always-resurgent metaphysical ambiguity.

5 ACCORD

Hegel deals with the problem of harmony in various sections of his *Lectures on Aesthetics*. In his initial comments on the concept of harmony, which appear precisely in the pages concerning music, we already have a systematic view held together by observations on abstract beauty that exhibits regularity, symmetry, and conformity to law. Harmony is defined as a relationship among qualitative differences or, rather, the totality of these differences grounded in the essence of the thing itself.

According to this interpretation, such a relationship eludes conformity with principle in that harmony contains within itself regular features, but it advances beyond the notion of equal measure and the repetition of these features. At the same time, qualitative differences present themselves as not only differences in the context of opposition and contradiction but also a congruous unity that highlights all the moments that pertain to it and that it unifies organically. Harmony consists in the totality of essential aspects with their oppositions dissolved; as a result, their associations and inner connections manifest themselves as unity. It is in this sense that, Hegel explains, we speak of the harmony of shapes, colours, and notes; and so blue, yellow, green, and red are necessary differences in colour contained in the essence of colour itself. Unlike symmetry, where we have only differences joined together regularly in an external unity, here we also have direct oppositions, for example yellow and blue, as well as their neutralization and concrete identity. The beauty of the harmony of colours consists in the elimination of difference and opposition, such that the consonance of the differences themselves emerges. They are related to one another because colour is not a one-sided but essential totality. Goethe says that the demand for such totality can go so far that if the eye looks upon a particular colour it subjectively sees other colours. Hegel then offers us a comparison to explain this fact. In music the tonic, subdominant, and dominant notes are essential differences in a sound harmonized in a unified whole. There is consonance in their differences. We encounter this in the harmony of the human figure as well: its position, whether in a state of rest or movement; no difference should appear one-sidedly by itself because the harmony would be destroyed. Hegel concludes this point by saying, however, that harmony as such is not yet subjectivity and the spirit, which are free and ideal. This is because in subjectivity and the spirit, "unity is not just association and an accord but a positing of differences negatively, whereby alone their ideal unity is established" (Hegel, 141; translated by Corrado Federici). Harmony does not achieve this ideality. For example, though they are all based on harmony, all melodies have in them and express a higher, freer subjectivity. In Hegel's view, "Mere harmony does not, in general, manifest either subjective animation as such or spirituality although it is the highest stage of abstract form and already approaches free subjectivity" (141).

6 RELATIONSHIP

The melody/harmony pairing is always in play. Prior to Hegel, Novalis theorized the existence of parallels between the senses and the arts on the basis of these two concepts. He pointed out the necessity of unity in the form of paintings, created by fixed relationships and similar to the unity of musical harmony. He also stated that harmony and melody are generally speaking one and the same thing. Melody is *successive*, while harmony is *relative*, with the added feature that harmony is the relationship between two or more simultaneous notes.

Out these observations there emerges an entire set of issues pertaining to description – issues that concern the evolution of aesthetic ideas, history and technology in the arts, and music theory in a comprehensive ensemble of conceptual interpretations, currents, poetics, and styles.

From the perspective of musicology, some have spoken of a crisis in the doctrine or doctrines of harmony, in light of recent revolutions in the world of art, technology, and thought. As Jean-Jacques Nattiez claims, "There are no musico-harmonic phenomena per se: they are accessible to us only because they have become the object of a *process of symbolization* that organizes them, makes them intelligible" (1990, 217).

This viewpoint is very important because it explains the fact that harmony in a particular period of music history or particular composer is understandable only through a metalanguage that accounts for it. We need only read a number of treatises produced in different countries and epochs to see that this is true. Jean-Philippe Rameau (2019) based his theoretical work on natural resonance, a theory that does not, however, explain perfect consonance in the minor triad in music. For this, nineteenth-century French composer Vincent d'Indy relied on the theory of resonance in the minor triad proposed by Gioseffo Zarlino in the sixteenth, one that is no longer based on the harmonic division but on the arithmetical division of the chord. In 1844 François-Joseph Fétis saw harmony as grounded in a natural law, setting the systems operating in folk music against the theory of tonality. But all these thinkers tend to consider their basic principles fundamental and, therefore, their own concepts to be absolutely definitive. For the purpose of clarifying the meaning of the term *harmony*, it seems that a phenomenological description is called for.

7 RHYTHM

In *Music and Discourse* (1990), Nattiez suggests that studies on harmony seem to correspond, depending on the point of view, to the composer's "strategies of production" and his mental categories, which explain the organization of the work (the *poietic* perspective), the way harmonious phenomena are perceived (the *extensional* perspective), or description The procedure includes a taxonomic analysis of what the composer is doing, without considering the problem of the poietic or aesthetic relevance of the facts identified (the neutral or *material* perspective). Even when these aspects are not explicitly thematized, different theories always tend to justify their own positions as they adopt the poietic criterion, the aesthetic criterion, or both. Nattiez adds that near the end of his *Treatise on Harmony* (1722) Rameau admits that knowledge is not sufficient for perfection if it is not aided by good taste, and that we have no rules for determining good taste except variety in the composition (the criterion here is essentially extensional in that it is based on the effect of a given sequence of notes). For d'Indy, the consonances *result* from melodic movements (here the criterion is implicitly poietic), and other examples could be cited.

In truth, music has several parameters: harmonic, melodic, rhythmical, and others that in different epochs have different degrees of importance. Like writers and artists of the nineteenth and twentieth centuries, contemporary composers upset the balance among the different points of view. Essentially, the wisdom of the existing theories of harmony is not being questioned here; I am merely attempting to point out that the formulation of a theory of harmony concerns the perspective of the poietic, the aesthetic, and the material, as well as their combinations.

It is possible to identify several correspondences, as we find in the complex theory of harmony advanced by Marius Schneider (1970), who compares the myths and traditions of different cultures.

According to Iamblichus, Apollo and Pythagoras revealed to the world the harmony of the spheres and the music that it inspired. The Pythagoreans thought highly of the tetractys for two reasons: first, because it reflected the essential structure of nature and explained the laws of both the music of the heavens and the music created by humans as a function of harmony; second, because it allowed for the conceptualization of a music capable of imitating the harmony of the heavenly spheres and so aspired to union with the divine. The importance of the tetractys was further underscored by the fact that music was given a cathartic function directed at the moral and religious improvement of the individual.

8 PERFECTION

According to Pythagorean philosophers, there exists a harmony of the soul since according to this concept the soul was the harmony of the body, that is to say, the harmonious and mathematical relationship among the material parts of the body as regards their proportions and the tension among them. Plato, who has this theory expounded by Simmias in the *Phaedo*, rejects that interpretation of harmony because it subordinates the existence of the soul in terms of its duration to that of the body (tuning a musical instrument is possible only with that particular instrument and is contained in it). However, he preserves and develops the idea of proportional relations among the parts of the soul (*Phaedrus*). An entire tradition that combines elements of

Pythagoreanism and Platonism accepted the idea of the inner music of a finely tuned soul. The ugly soul corresponds to a musical instrument either counterfeit or poorly tuned. In both the *Theaetetus* and the *Timaeus*, Plato identifies a whole series of operations "analogous" to the creation of musical harmony identified by the Pythagoreans as the model of perfect harmony: for instance, uniting elements using as a criterion eurhythmy, based on the analogy of forms and on architectural surfaces and masses (a problem taken up by Vitruvius); or inserting the middle term in a syllogism (on this point, see the theories of the golden ratio). Dealing in particular with the rhythm of the soul of the world, in the *Timaeus* (34b–36d), Plato makes use of the double musical tetractys of the Pythagoreans – $(1 + 3 + 5 + 7) + (2 + 4 + 6 + 8) = 36$, the sum of the first four odd numbers and the first four even numbers – to obtain the celestial spectrum whose notes allow the orchestration of the harmony of the spheres. The influence of these passages from the *Timaeus* on Western thought has been enormous. They describe in turn the correlation between the rhythm of the soul of the world and that of the human soul in the context of philosophy (the theory of the macrocosm and the microcosm), aesthetics (the canon of divine proportions in Luca Pacioli and Leonardo da Vinci), and science (the discovery of the laws of planetary motion by Johannes Kepler and the formulation of the golden ratio). The concept of harmony as a numerical relationship indeed became fused from the beginning with other ideas and practices, for example, those pertaining to medicine (Hippocrates) and astronomy, as mentioned. It is worth repeating that harmony consists in a relationship that brings together different parts to form a whole, or, if we prefer, it consists in the balanced resolution of opposite forces that according to the Heraclitian tradition compose themselves in such a way that this union forms a coherent whole that satisfies the spirit and the senses. This ancient meaning was maintained for more than two millennia. The proportions of the whole are fundamental elements for the success of a work. This idea influenced interpretations that became increasingly more detailed in music and the arts.

9 BALANCE

We can appreciate the impact of the aesthetic concept implied by the preceding observations. According to an ancient maxim on harmony, we can find a wonderful synthesis of every subsequent argument in the unfolding of changing traditions throughout history, from the admiration of nature to the perceptual and compositional order of the arts, and from the inventive imagination to reception. "Harmony is generally the result of contraries, for it is the unity of multiplicity and the agreement of discordances," is a statement made by Philolaus (fragment DK 3). The maxim indicates that the Greeks knew how to identify harmony in discordance by introducing the concept of control over what is contrary. Making concordant what is not offers us the image of a paradoxical theme (the Romans would term it *concordia discors*) and represents the system of contraries harmoniously unified. Harmony, then, illustrates an idea of wholeness that prevails over dissonances and in a mythological interpretation marks the end of chaos and the affirmation of an orderly vision of the cosmos. This theory is the foundation of all the aesthetic elements and with its focus on numbers and sequences from antiquity to the present day, it influences for good or ill not only many examples of works related to classicism but also, surprisingly, many recent experiments advanced by the avant-garde. We have already encountered observations such as these in our discussion of Hegel. This inevitably involves the aesthetic revolution of the twentieth century. Dorfles (1986) proposes a theory of disharmony which is in fact well suited to modern art from a historical and cultural perspective. Modern art was the product of an anti-classical imagination; it attempted to place the emphasis on the power of shock, provocation, distraction, and the ugly, as opposed to the idea of balance, symmetry, serenity, beauty, and grace. The importance assigned to dissonance and randomness in the last century limited the role that harmony and symmetry played in history and aesthetic theory.

The modern meaning of polyphonic harmony concerns the relationship between simultaneous notes and, more particularly, a sequence of chords. Music, therefore, has a two-dimensional quality: the simultaneity of different notes and the succession of these notes. As a form of musical writing, harmony replaces the precedents beginning in the Renaissance. Due to a series of processes related to its transformation and its development, music enters a presumed golden age with the invention of the sonata and the symphony. Its relationship with time is expressed by the dominant and tonic scales, which create instability that resolves itself in the rest of the second element (the tonic rest). For more than two centuries, musical aesthetics is tied to this concept, which undergoes a crisis in the twentieth century.

From the foregoing comments, we can understand the technical and symbolic reach of the notion of harmony, from physics to metaphysics, from music to architecture and literature. In addition, we have been able to establish that it places the subjective world in relation to the objective one. This is because harmony studies movement in relation to space and time.

10 CONJUNCTIONS

The notion of harmony can also be applied to painting and architecture if analyzed from the point of view of interrelations among the arts. This is a matter of dividing space in accordance with the proportions in which consonant musical intervals divide the octave. The idea of a harmony of colours, analogous to musical harmony, may have a scientific basis. Isaac Newton discovered the possibility of separating white light into its component colours by using a prism, and he identified the resulting rainbow by analogy to the Phrygian scale; the spectral continuum could be divided according to any desired proportion. The idea of a *harmony of colours*, analogous to musical harmony, can indeed be based on science if we calculate the relationships among the colours of the light spectrum, which correspond to the relationships among the musical notes. It must be noted, however, that at times we find real relationships and at other times the correspondence is merely metaphorical.

The theory of tempo, duration, movement, and simultaneity can also exist in both the visual and the plastic arts. The distinction often made between the arts of time (music, dance, theatre, cinema, and poetry) and the arts of space (architecture, sculpture, painting, and drawing) is only an apparent one. The temporal arts are distinguished from the others by the ways in which duration is shaped: apparent time pertains to an aesthetic principle that is inherent in the work itself. But in the visual and plastic arts, duration's actual role is not less important, though it intervenes more freely. If we wanted to find an example of *agitato* (very quick and with excitement) in painting, we could cite Sandro Botticelli's *Calumny*, where the figures seem to move with a particular intensity and tension. The image in a painting does not presuppose any rule, order, or predetermined sequence. The time taken to contemplate the image is determined solely by the viewer's disposition, in spite of the duration inscribed in the image by the artist. For these reasons, the notion of harmony is always of fundamental importance for the technical and structural aspects of the arts. Correspondingly, we can find instances of musical harmony in architecture and painting from the Renaissance on. Space was divided into the same proportions as consonant musical intervals divide the octave, as stated above.

11 DURATION

If we conduct a comparative analysis, we discover that time is part of the equation in architecture. In this art form we have a true duration in the act of contemplation. There are temples that were planned taking into account the seasons and the sun's path across the sky, such that sunlight illuminates the different parts of the temple in the course of the day. The interior also exhibits changing optical effects as the gaze falls upon the directional-force lines of the architectural elements, modulations, and soaring vertical lines, in a word, the effects of these material tensions. A perfect example of this phenomenon is Chartres Cathedral. There are also other features relevant to our discussion, such as the dramatic opening up of space, dynamic intensity, or feeling of exaltation, pensiveness, peace, and restfulness. The solicitation of these feelings and the expression of forces and materials are evident in the variety of architectural styles. The upward thrust, which is more or less prominent, represents a musical agogic accent in architecture. In this case the gothic is an illuminating example. We experience a striking impression of acceleration in works executed in the flamboyant or flowery gothic style, whereas the Greek temples seem to inspire a sense of calm and serenity. The suggestion of movement noted above is also, in part, related to the notion of harmony. This is implicit in the same lines of directional force. We can find a corresponding process in painting and sculpture, where the artist strives to create the appearance of balance and symmetry. As regards the notion of symmetry, which leads us to consider notions of spatialized time and simultaneity of perceptual data, we once again have the themes of movement and rhythm. Standing in opposition to Goethe's theory of architecture as "rigidified" music, Schopenhauer states, "Rhythm is in time as symmetry is in space." With this concept in mind, we can consider a piece of music as symmetrical division and subdivision, beats and fractions of beats (i.e., musical signature), and note that this same piece is closely linked with and contained in the whole, precisely as in a symmetrical building (*The World as Will and Representation*, supplements to book 3, chapter 39). At this point, we are in a position to understand that the parallel drawn between music and architecture, on the basis of a distinction between the temporal and the spatial arts, is not as clear-cut as it may seem. It is important to connect the concept of movement and rhythm with that of symmetry, and to recognize the extent to which these two notions come into contact with each other. This is demonstrated by discussions on the issues of harmony and disharmony, assonance and dissonance, and respect for rules vs. freedom of feeling within the historical framework of the liberal arts and the fine arts. What we have here is a line of development that extends all the way from Pythagoras to us and includes St Augustine and Leibniz. In *De architectura* (book 10), Vitruvius examines the problems of proportion using as an example a row of columns spaced evenly: an analysis that highlights the interplay between symmetry and harmony. In the present study, harmony emerges as an indisputable category relative to true proportion, reception, and function. This theme, which embraces both measure and number, the whole and the parts, the cosmos and the human body, reappears in later studies up to Leon Battista Alberti (*De re aedificatoria* [On the art of building]), Albrecht Dürer (*On Human Proportion*), and Andrea Palladio (*I quattro libri dell'architettura* [The four books on architecture]). The evolution of an aesthetics of harmony would be translated into the dilemma of Romantic poetics and then dissolve in the poetics of the twentieth century.

12 CONSTRUCTIONS

In conclusion, the following distinction has been made in our study of the concept of harmony: In general terms, it is unity in multiplicity, a kind of order consisting of the fact that different parts and their functions converge, without contrasts, to produce the same overall effect or felicitous combination of different elements. In specific terms, it is the aesthetic aspect of the sensation produced when we hear multiple sounds simultaneously. Furthermore, harmony involves an entire system of thought and techniques related to movement and simultaneity. When considering a piece of music, after expressing a judgment based on ideas of the beautiful, sublime, and graceful, there arises the need to expand on our evaluation. We must, therefore, formulate other judgments relative to rhythm, in order to understand the piece better and to analyze its salient features. Slowness or speed evoke emotions and feelings, and they modulate the listener's state of mind, but harmony manifests itself beyond the implementation of agogic accents and casts its gaze into the future.

Contemplation and harmony come together in the search for an improved human condition. The word contemplation derives from the Latin verb *contemplare*, the root of which is the noun *templum*, meaning a space marked out for observing auguries and omens. From this comes the idea of contemplation as an activity of the spirit in which the subject dissolves into the object while interpreting it, thus revealing itself in state of quiet and repose. This meaning of contemplation is very close to that of the Greek term *theoria*. According to Diogenes Laertes, when

Anaxagoras claims that the value of life is determined by knowing how to contemplate the sky, the sun, and the moon, he highlights the relationship between human perception and the natural order. In the same vein, we have the views of Plato and Aristotle, as cited above. This disposition of the mind and the faculties of perceptions can be found frequently throughout history, and among the philosophers who discuss it from the aesthetic stand-point a special insight comes from Jean-Jacques Rousseau when he speaks of contemplative souls who love to be intoxicated by the beauties of nature, described as a spectacle: "The more sensi-tive a soul the contemplator has, the more he gives himself up to the ecstasies this harmony arouses in him. A sweet and deep reverie takes possession of his senses then, and through a delicious intoxication he loses himself in the immensity of this beautiful system, with which he feels himself one" (Rousseau 1992, 92).

In contemplation and harmony, we are all Rousseau's children. Today, we cannot avoid meditating on nature's artistry in the context of a culture of contemplation.

Harmony sends us a double signal: the fear that the classical will disappear and the necessity of rediscovering the aura in the contemporary era. Some artists today articulate this fear and this necessity in works that aim to ensure the survival of antiquity.

References

Agamben, Giorgio. 2009. *Il regno e la gloria. Per una genealogia teologica dell'economia e del governo, Homo sacer* II, 2. Turin: Bollati Boringhieri. Translated by Lorenzo Chiesa as *The Kingdom and the Glory: For a Theological Genealogy of Economy and Government* (2010).

— 2019. *Il regno e il giardino*. Venice: Neri Pozza. Translated by Adam Kotsko as *The Kingdom and the Garden* (2010).

Albert, C. 2000. "Harmonie" (Harmony). In *Ästhetische Grundbegriffe*, edited by Karlheinz Barck, Martin Fortius, Freidrich Wolfzettel, and Burkhart Steinwachs, 1–23. Vol. 3 of *Historisches Wörterbuch in sieben Bändem*. Stuttgart-Weimar: Verlag J.B. Metzer.

Alberti, Leon Battista. 1966. *L'architettura*. Italian translation by G. Orlandi. Milan: Il Polifilo. Originally published as *De re aedificatoria*.

Aristotle. 1980. *The Nicomachean Ethics*. Translated by William David Ross. Oxford: Oxford University Press.

— 2020. *Poetics*. Perseus Digital Library. Tufts University.

Arnheim, Rudolf. 1974. *Pensiero visivo*. Turin: Einaudi. Originally published as *Visual Thinking* (1969).

Assunto, Rosario. 1973. *L'antichità come futuro* (Antiquity as future). Milan: Mursia.

— 2005. *Il paesaggio e l'estetica* (The landscape and aesthetics). Palermo: Novecento.

Augé, Marc. 2004. *Rovine e macerie. Il senso del tempo* (Ruins and rubble: The sense of time). Turin: Bollati Boringhieri.

Bakhtin, Mikhail. 2001. *Estetica e romanzo* (Aesthetics and the novel). Turin: Einaudi.

Balthasar, Hans Urs von. 1975–86. *Gloria. Un'estetica teologica* (Glory: A theological aesthetics). 7 vols. Milan: Jaca Book. Originally published in German (1961–69).

Baltrušaitis, Jurgis. 1973. *Medioevo fantastico. Antichità ed esotismo nell'arte gotica* (The fantastic in the Middle Ages: Antiquity and the exotic in gothic art). Milan: Adelphi.

– 1978. *Anamorfosi o magia artificiale degli effetti meravigliosi* (Anamorphosis or artificial magic of marvellous effects). Milan: Adelphi.

– 1999. *Risvegli e prodigi. La metamorfosi del gotico* (Awakenings and wonders: The metamorphosis of the gothic). Milan: Adelphi.

Balzac, Honoré de. 1899. "Seraphita," in *The Works of Balzac*, translated by Katharine Prescott Wormeley. Centenary edition, *La Comédie Humaine of Honoré de Balzac: Philosophical Studies*, vol. 28, *Seraphita, The Alkahest*. Boston: Little, Brown.

Barthes, Roland. 1977. "Diritto negli occhi" (Straight in the eye). In Roland Barthes, *L'ovvio e l'ottuso* (The obvious and the obtuse), 301–6. Turin: Einaudi, 1985.

– 1985. *L'ovvio e l'ottuso* (The obvious and the obtuse). Turin: Einaudi.

Battisti, Eugenio. 1962. *L'Antirinascimento* (The anti-Renaissance). Milan: Feltrinelli.

Baudrillard, Jean. 1981. *Simulacres et simulation* (Simulacra and simulation). Paris: Galilée.

Bauman, Zygmunt. 2017. *Retrotopia*. Rome-Bari: Laterza.

Belting, Hans. 2010. *I canoni dello sguardo. Storia della cultura visiva tra Oriente e Occidente.* (The canons of the gaze: History of visual culture in the East and West). Turin: Bollati Boringhieri.

– 2017. *Specchio del mondo* (The mirror of the world). Rome: Carocci.

Benassi, Stefano. 1995. *Gli antichi e le origini del moderno. Modelli estetici tra letteratura e arti figurative* (The ancients and the origins of the modern sensibility: Aesthetic models from literature and the figurative arts). Bologna: Clueb.

Benjamin, Walter. 1966. *L'opera d'arte nell'epoca della sua riproduzione tecnica.* Turin: Einaudi. Translated in English as "The Work of Art in the Age of Mechanical Reproduction."

Berque, Augustin. 2010. *Milieu et identité humanie. Notes sur le dépassement de la modernité* (Milieu and human identity: Notes on surpassing modernity). Paris: Donner lieu.

Binik, Oriana. 2019. *Quando il crimine è sublime* (When the crime is sublime). Milan: Mimesis.

Birkoff, George David. 1933. *Aesthetic Measure*. Cambridge, MA: Harvard University Press.

Bloom, Harold. 1996. *Il canone occidentale*. Milan: Bompiani. Originally published as *The Western Canon* (1994).

Blumenberg, Hans. 1969. *Paradigmi per una metaforologia*. Bologna: Il Mulino. Published in English as *Paradigms for a Metaphorology* (1969).

– 2010. *Teoria dell'inconcettualità* (A theory of non-conceptuality). Palermo: Due punti.

Boardman, John. 2004. *Archeologia della nostalgia. Come i Greci reinventarono il loro passato* Milan: Bruno Mondadori. Published in English as *The Archaeology of Nostalgia: How the Greeks Re-created Their Mythical Past* (2002).

Boccali, Giuliano. 2017. "Immagini della natura nella poesia indiana classica" (Images of nature in classical Indian poetry). *Il Verri* 2: 34–47.

Boitani, Piero. 2004. *Parole alate* (Winged words). Milan: Mondadori.

Bredekamp, Horst. 2015. *Immagini che ci guardano. Teoria dell'atto iconico*. Milan: Cortina. Translated by Elizabeth Clegg as *Image Acts: A Systematic Approach to Visual Agency* (2021).

Caillois, Roger. 1984. *Nel cuore del fantastico* (The heart of the fantastic). Milan: Feltrinelli. Originally published as *Au cœur du fantastique* (Paris: Gallimard, 1965).

– 2001. *Man and the Sacred*. Translated by Meyer Barash. Urbana: Illinois University Press. Originally published as *L'homme et le sacré* (Paris: Leroux, 1939).

Canetti, Elias. 1981. *Massa e potere* (Crowds and power). Milan: Adelphi.

Carchia, Gianni. 2000. *L'amore del pensiero* (The love of thinking). Macerata: Quodlibet.

Castells, Manuel. 2002. *Galassia Internet* (Internet galaxy). Oxford: Oxford University Press.

Cattaneo, Francesco. 2019. *La presenza degli dei. Filosofia e mito in Friedrich Nietzsche e Walter F. Otto tra verità e bellezza* (The presence of the gods: Between truth and beauty in philosophy and myth in Friedrich Nietzsche and Walter F. Otto). Salerno-Naples: Orthotes.

Centanni, Monica. 2006. "Malinconica Polimnia. La 'Musa pensosa' come figura del pathos dell'intellettuale" (Melancholy Polyhymnia: The "pensive muse" as symbol of the pathos of the intellectual). In *Musa pensosa* (Pensive muse), catalogue of the Colosseum exhibit, edited by Angelo Bottini, 151–62. Milan: Electa.

Chateaubriand, François-René de. 1813. *The Beauties of Christianity*. Translated by Frederic Shoberl. London: Henry Colburn. Published as *Le Génie du christianisme* (1802).

Chiodo, Simona. 2008. *La rappresentazione. Una risposta filosofica sulla verità dell'esperienza sensibile* (Representation: A philosophical essay on the truth of sensible experience). Milan: Bruno Mondadori.

Chuang-tzu. 1998. *Il vero libro di Nan-hua* (The book of Nan-hua). Milan: Mondadori.

Colli, Giorgio. 1969. *Filosofia dell'espressione* (Philosophy of expression). Milan: Adelphi.

Coomaraswamy, Ananda Kentish. 1987. *Induismo e buddhismo*. 2nd ed. Milan: Rusconi. Published as *Hinduism and Buddhism* (1943).

Corbin, Alain. 2016. *Histoire du silence. De la Renaissance à nos jours* (History of silence: From the Renaissance to the present). Paris: Albin Michel.

Creuzer, Friedrich. 2004. *Simbolica e mitologia 1810–1812* (Symbolism and mythology 1810–12). Rome: Edizioni Riuniti.

Danto, Arthur. 2007. *Dopo la morte dell'arte*. Milan: Mondadori. Published as *After the End of Art* (1997).

– 2010. *La destituzione filosofica dell'arte*. Palermo: Aesthetica. Published as *The Philosophical Disenfranchisement of Art* (1986).

Debord, Guy. 1967. *La Societé du spectacle*. Paris: Editions Buchet-Chastel. Translated by Ken Knabb as *The Society of the Spectacle* (2014).

Demetrio, Duccio. 2012. *I sensi del silenzio* (The meanings of silence). Milan: Mimesis.

Derrida, Jacques. 2005. *La verità in pittura*. Milan: Newton-Compton. Published as *The Truth in Painting* (1978).

Dorfles, Gillo. (1959) 1971. *Il divenire delle arti* (The becoming of the arts). Turin: Einaudi.

– 1986. *Elogio della disarmonia* (In praise of disharmony). Milan: Garzanti.

Duso, Giuseppe. 2016. *La rappresentazione politica. Genesi e crisi del concetto* (Political representation: Genesis and crisis of the concept). Milan: Angeli.

Eliade, Mircea. 1999. *Trattato di storia delle religioni* (Treatise on the history of religions). Turin: Bollati Boringhieri.

Emo, Andrea. 1992. *Le voci delle Muse. Saggi sulla religione e l'arte, 1918–1981* (The voices of the muses: Essays on religion and art, 1918–81). Venice: Marsilio.

Fétis, François-Joseph. 2008. *Complete Treatise on the Theory and the Practice of Harmony*. Translated by Peter M. Landey. Hillsdale, NY: Pendragon Press. Originally published as *Traité complet de la théorie et de la pratique de l'harmonie* (Paris: Maurice Schlesinger, 1844).

Florensky, Pavel. 1977. *Le porte regali. Saggio sull'icona* (Royal doors: An essay on the icon). Milan: Adelphi.

– 2018. *The Pillar and the Ground of Truth*. Translated by Boris Jakim. Princeton, NJ: Princeton University Press.

Focillon, Henri. 1987. *Vita delle forme*. Turin: Einaudi. Published as *The Life of Forms in Art* (1942).

Foucault, Michel. 2008. *Utopie Eterotopie* (Utopias and heterotopias). Naples: Cronopio.

– 2011. *Spazi altri* (Of other spaces). Milan: Mimesis.

Francastel, Pierre. 1958. *Lo spazio figurativo dal Rinascimento al cubismo* (Figurative space from the Renaissance to cubism). Turin: Einaudi.

Freedberg, David. 1993. *Il potere delle immagini*. Turin: Einaudi. Published as *The Power of Images* (1957).

Freud, Sigmund. 2014. *Freud Verbatim: Quotations and Aphorisms*. Translated by Christopher Barber. London: Overlook Duckworth.

Gadamer, Hans-Georg. 2000. *Verità e metodo*. Milan: Bompiani. Published as *Truth and Method* (1960).

Genette, Gérard. (1966–72) 1969–76. *Figures I, II, II*. Turin: Einaudi.

Gil, F. 1980. "Rappresentazione" (Representation). In *Enciclopedia Einaudi*, edited by Ruggiero Romano, 346–81. Vol. 11. Turin: Einaudi.

Givone, Sergio. 1995. *Storia del nulla* (The history of nothingness). Rome-Bari: Laterza.

– 2017. *L'infinito* (The infinite). Bologna: Il Mulino.

Goethe, Johann Wolfgang von. 1983. *Massime e riflessioni* (Maxims and reflections). 2 vols. Edited by S. Seidel. Rome-Naples: Theoria.

Gombrich, Ernst. 1965. *Arte e illusion*. Turin: Einaudi. Published as *Art and Illusion* (1960).

– 1984. *Il senso dell'ordine*. Turin: Einaudi. Published as *The Sense of Order: A Study in the Psychology of Decorative Art* (1979).

Grassi, Luigi, and Mario Pepe. 1994. *Dizionario dei termini artistici* (Dictionary of art terms). Milan: Tea/Mondadori.

Griffero, Tonino. 2010. *Atmosferologia. Estetica degli spazi emozionali* (Atmospherology: The aesthetics of emotional space). Milan: Mimesi.

Hamann, Johann Georg. 1938. *Scritti e frammenti estetici*. Edited by S. Lupi. Florence: Sansoni.

Haugeland, John. 1988. *Intelligenza artificiale*. Turin: Bollati Boringhieri. Published as *Artificial Intelligence* (1985).

Hegel, Georg Wilhelm Friedrich. 1997. *Estetica*. Edited by Nicolao Marker. Translated by Nicolao Merker and Nicola Vaccaro. Turin: Einaudi. Translated by T.M. Knox as *Aesthetics: Lectures on Fine Art* (1975).

Heidegger, Martin. 1971. "The Thing." In *Poetry, Language, Thought*, translated by Alfred Hofstader, 163–80. New York: Harper & Row.

Henry, Albert. 1971. *Metonomia e metafora* (Metonymy and metaphor). Turin: Einaudi.

Hildebrand, Alfred von. 1907. *The Problem of Form in Painting and Sculpture*. New York: G.E. Stechert. Originally published in German as *Das Problem der Form in der bildenden Kunst*. Strasbourg: J.H. Ed. Heitz, 1893.

Huizinga, Johan. (1943) 2004. *Lo scempio del mondo* (The waning of the world). Edited by Lucio Villari. Milan: Mondadori.

Husserl, Edmund. 1965. *Idee per una fenomenologia pura e per una fenomenologia filosofica* (Ideas for a pure phenomenology and for a philosophical phenomenology). Edited by Enrico Filippini. Turin: Einaudi.

– 1968. *Meditazioni cartesiane* (Cartesian meditations). Edited by F. Costa. Milan: Bompiani.

Iamblichus. 1991. *On the Pythagorean Life*. Atlanta: Scholars Press.

Jakobson, Roman. 1973. *Questions de poétique* (Questions of poetics). Paris: Seuil.

Jaspers, Karl. 1950. *Psicologia delle visioni del mondo* (The psychology of worldviews). Rome: Astrolabio.

Jonze, Spike, dir. *Her*. 2013. Burbank, CA: Warner Bros.

Jung, Carl Gustav. 2010. *Il Libro Rosso* (The red book). Edited by Sonu Shamdasani. Turin: Bollati Boringhieri.

Kandel, Eric R. 2017. *Arte e neuroscienza. Le due culture a confronto*. Milan: Cortina. Published as *Reductionism in Art and Brain Science: Bridging the Two Cultures* (2016).

Kant, Immanuel. 1979. *Critica del giudizio*. Edited by Alfredo Gargiulo. Revised by V. Verra. Rome-Bari: Laterza. Translated in English as *Critique of Judgment*.

Kerényi, Károly. 1979. *Miti e misteri* (Myths and mysteries). Turin: Bollati Boringhieri.

Köhler, Wolfgang. 1969. *The Task of Gestalt Psychology*. Princeton, NJ: Princeton University Press.

Kracauer, Siegfried. 1982. *Le masse come ornamento* (Crowds as ornament). Naples: Prismi.

Lanier, Jaron. 2019. *L'alba del nuovo tutto. Il futuro della realtà virtuale* (The dawning of the new everything: The future of virtual reality). Milan: Il Saggiatore.

Latour, Bruno. 2013. *Cogitamus. Sei lettere sull'umanesimo scientifico* (Cogitamus: Six letters on scientific humanism). Bologna: Il Mulino.

Le Breton, David. 2018a. *Il sapore del mondo. Un'antropologia dei sensi* (Sensing the world: An anthropology of the senses). Milan: Cortina.

– 2018b. *Sul silenzio* (On silence). Milan: Cortina.

Leopardi, Giacomo. 1977. *Zibaldone* (Notebook). Rome: Newton-Compton.

Leroi-Gourhan, André. 1993. *Il gesto e la parola*. 2 vols. Turin: Einaudi. Translated by Anna Bostock Berger as *Gesture and Speech* (1995).

Lévinas, Emmanuel. 1980. *Totalità e infinito*. Milan: Jaca Book. Published as *Totality and Infinity* (1961).

Levinson, Barry, dir. 1994. *Disclosure*. Burbank, CA: Warner Bros.

Lévi-Strauss, Claude. 1984. *Lo sguardo da lontano* (The view from afar). Turin: Einaudi. Originally published as *Le regard éloigné*.

– 1994. *Guardare, ascoltare, leggere*. Milan: Il Saggiatore. Published as *Look, Listen, Read* (1993).

Lipps, Theodor. 1997. "Estetica" (Aesthetics). In *Estetica e empatia* (Aesthetics and empathy), edited by Andrea Pinotti, 117–218. Milan: Guerini.

Löwith, Karl. 2018. *Sul senso della storia* (Meaning in history). Milan: Mimesis.

Luhmann, Niklas. 2000. *Art as a Social System*. Translated by Eva M. Knodt. Princeton, NJ: Princeton University Press.

Lyotard, Jean-François. 1981. *La condizione postmoderna*. Milan: Feltrinelli. Published as *The Postmodern Condition* (1979).

– 1998. "Anamnèse du visible II" (Anamnesis of the visible II). *Bulletin de la Société française d'Esthétique* 16, no. 2: 1–8.

McEwan, Ian. 2019. *Machines Like Me*. London: Jonathan Cape.

Maldonado, Tomás. 1992. *Reale e virtuale* (The real and the virtual). Milan: Feltrinelli.

Majewski, Lech, dir. 2011. *The Mill and the Cross*. Warsaw: Telewizja Polska.

Mallgrave, Harry Francis. 2013. *L'empatia degli spazi*. Milan: Cortina. Published as *Empathy, Form, and Space* (1994).

Merleau-Ponty, Maurice. 1962. *Senso e non senso*. Milan: Garzanti. Published as *Sense and Non-sense* (1992).

– 1984. *La prosa del mondo* (The prose of the world). Rome: Editori Riuniti.

Milani, Raffaele. 2008. *I volti della grazia*. Bologna: Il Mulino. Published as *The Aesthetics of Grace* (2013).

Moles, Abraham, and Elisabeth Rohmer. 1985. *Labirinti del vissuto. Tipologia dello spazio e immagini della comunicazione* (Labyrinths of lived spaces: A typology of space and images of communication). Venice: Marsilio.

Montani, Pietro. 2014. *Tecnologie della sensibilità. Estetica e immaginazione interattiva* (The technology of sensibility: Aesthetics and the interactive imagination). Milan: Cortina.

Morin, Edgar. 2016. *Pour une crisologie*. Paris: L'Herne.

Nagel, Thomas. 2015. *Mente e cosmo* (Mind and cosmos). Milan: Cortina.

Nancy, Jean-Luc. 2014. *Il corpo dell'arte* (The body of art). Milan: Mimesis.

Natoli, Salvatore. 2019. *L'animo degli offesi e il contagio del male* (The spirit of the harmed and the contagion of evil). Milan: Il Saggiatore.

Nattiez, Jean-Jacques. 1990. *Music and Discourse: Toward a Semiotics of Music*. Translated by Carolyn Abbate. Princeton, NJ: Princeton University Press.

Nietzsche, Friedrich Wilhelm. 2016. "The Spirit of Gravity." In *Thus Spake Zarathustra*, Project Gutenberg E-book, translated by Thomas Common.

Novalis. 1993. *Opera filosofica* (Philosophical writings). Edited by Giampiero Moretti. Turin: Einaudi.

Palladio, Andrea. 1981. *Scritti sull'architettura (1554–1579)* (Writings on architecture, 1554–70). Edited by Lionello Puppi. Vicenza: Neri Pozza.

Panofsky, Erwin. 1962. *Studi di iconologia*. Turin: Einaudi. Published as *Studies in Iconology* (1939).

Pareyson, Luigi. 1988. *Estetica. Teoria della formatività* (Aesthetics: A theory of formativity). Milan: Bompiani.

Parsons, Talcott. 1971. *The System of Modern Societies*. Englewood Cliffs, NJ: Prentice-Hall.

Pinotti, Andrea, ed. 1997. *Estetica e empatia* (Aesthetics and empathy). Milan: Guerini.

Plato. n.d. *Protagoras*. Perseus Digital Library. Tufts University.

– n.d. *Republic*. Perseus Digital Library. Tufts University.

Plotinus. *The Six Enneads*. The Internet Classics Archive. Accessed 15 September 2021. http://classics.mit.edu/Plotinus/enneads.1.first.html.

Pollitt, Jerome Jordan. 1974. *The Ancient View of Greek Art: Criticism, History, and Terminology*. New Haven, CT: Yale University Press.

Ponsoldt, James, dir. 2017. *The Circle*. Burbank, CA: STX Entertainment.

Portinaro, Pier Paolo. 2017. *L'imperativo di uccidere. Genocidio e democidio nella storia* (The imperative to kill: Genocide and democide in history). Rome-Bari: Laterza.

Prete, Antonio. 2016. *Grammatica dell'interiorità* (A grammar of interiority). Turin: Bollati Boringhieri.

Prince, Gerald. 1984. *Narratologia*. Parma: Pratiche. Published as *Narratology: The Forms and Functioning of Narrative* (1982).

Principe, Quirino. 2019. *Il fantasma dell'Opera. Sognando una filosofia* (The phantom of the opera: Dreaming a philosophy). Milan: Jaca Book.

Rameau, Jean-Philippe. 2019. *Trattato di armonia ricondotta ai suoi principi naturali* (Treatise on harmony). Milan: Edigeo. Published as *Traité de l'harmonie réduit à ses principes naturels* (1722).

Richards, Robert R., ed. 2002. *The Romantic Conception of Life: Science and Philosophy in the Age of Goethe*. Chicago: University of Chicago Press.

Richer, Jean. 1989. *Geografia sacra del mondo Greco* (Sacred geography of the Greek world). Milan: Rusconi.

Ricoeur, Paul 1986–88. *Tempo e racconto*. 3 vols. Milan: Jaca Book. Published as *Time and Narrative* (1983).

– 2016. "Architecture and Narrativity." *Études Ricoeuriennes/Ricoeur Studies* 7, no. 2: 31–42.

Rorty, Richard. 2004. *La filosofia e lo specchio della natura*. Milan: Bompiani. Published as *Philosophy and the Mirror of Nature* (1979).

Rousseau, Jean-Jacques. 1992. *The Reveries of the Solitary Walker*. Translated by Charles E. Butterworth. Indianapolis: Hackett.

Ruskin, John. 1988. *Pittori moderni*. Turin: Einaudi. Published as *Modern Painters* (1843).

Rykwert, Joseph. 1972. *La casa di Adamo in Paradiso*. Milan: Adelphi. Published as *On Adam's House in Paradise* (1972).

Saint Girons, Baldine. 2010. *L'atto estetico* (The aesthetic act). Modena: Mucchi.

Sartre, Jean-Paul. 1936. *L'imagination*. Paris: Alca. Published as *The Imagination* (1936).

– 1938. "Structure intentionelle de l'image" (The intentional structure of the image). *Revue de Métaphysique et de Morale* 45, no. 2: 71–89.

– 1966. *Che cos'è la letteratura?* Milan: Il Saggiatore. Published as *What Is Literature?* (1947).

– 2007. *L'immaginario: psicologia fenomenologica dell'immaginazione* (The imaginary: A phenomenological psychology of the imagination). Turin: Einaudi.

Sautoy, Marcus du. 2019. *The Creativity Code: Art and Innovation in the Age of AI.* Cambridge, MA: Harvard University Press.

Schaeffer, Jean-Marie. 2000. *The Art of the Modern Age: The Philosophy of Art from Kant to Heidegger.* Translated by Steven Randall. Princeton, NJ: Princeton University Press. Published as *L'art de l'âge moderne* (1992).

Schelling, Friedrich Wilhelm Joseph. 1986. *Filosofia dell'arte (1802–1803)* (The philosophy of art, 1802–03). Naples: Prismi.

Schlegel, August Wilhelm. 1977. *Corso di letteratura drammatica* (Lectures on dramatic literature). Genoa: Il Melangolo.

Schneider, Marius. 1970. *Il significato della musica* (The meaning of music). Milan: Rusconi.

Schopenhauer, Arthur. 1986. *Il mondo come volontà e rappresentazione.* Edited by P. Savj-Lopez and G. De Lorenzo. Rome-Bari: Laterza. Translated in English as *The World as Will and Representation* (1958).

– 2017. *Metafisica della natura* (The metaphysics of nature). Rome-Bari: Laterza.

Scott, Ridley, dir. 1982. *Blade Runner.* Burbank, CA: Warner Bros.

Searle, John R. 1994. *La riscoperta della mente.* Turin: Bollati Boringhieri. Published as *The Rediscovery of the Mind* (1992).

– 2018. *Vedere le cose come sono.* Milan: Cortina. Published as *Seeing Things as They Are: A Theory of Perception* (2015).

Sedlmayr, Hans. 1983. *Perdita del centro. Le arti figurative dei secoli XIX e XX come sintomo e simbolo di un'epoca.* Rome: Borla. Published as *Art in Crisis: The Lost Center* (2006).

Seneca, Lucius Annaeas. 1989. *Lettere a Lucilio* (Moral letters to Lucilius). Edited by U. Biella. Turin: UTET.

Settis, Salvatore. 2016. *Futuro del classico* (The future of the classic). Turin: Einaudi.

– 2020. *Modernità di Raffaello. Dalle lettere a Leone X alla Costituzione Italiana* (The modernity of Raphael: From the letters to Leo X to the Italian constitution). Rome: Scuderie del Quirinale.

Simmel, Georg. 1987a. "Il dominio della tecnica" (The dominance of technology). In *Tecnica e cultura* (Technology and culture), edited by Tomás Maldonado, 7–15. Milan: Feltrinelli.

– 1987b. "Le metropoli e la vita spirituale" (The metropolis and mental life). In *Tecnica e cultura* (Technology and culture), edited by Tomás Maldonado, 54–68. Milan: Feltrinelli.

Sloterdijk, Peter. 2017. *Che cosa è successo nel XX secolo* (What happened in the twentieth century). Turin: Bollati Boringhieri.

Souriau, Étienne. 1985. *La corrispondenza delle arti* (The correspondence of the arts). Florence: Alinea.

– 1989. *Vocabulaire d'esthétique* (A dictionary of aesthetics). Paris: Presses Universitaires de France.

Spielberg, Steven, dir. 2002. *A.I. Artificial Intelligence*. Burbank, CA: Warner Bros.

Spitzer, Leo. 1967. *L'armonia nel mondo. Storia semantica di un'idea* (The harmony of the world: A semantic history of an idea). Bologna: Il Mulino.

Starobinski, Jean. 2008. *Teoria del simbolo* (Theory of the symbol). Milan: Garzanti.

Stavru, Alessandro. 2011. *Il potere dell'apparenza. Percorso storico-critico nell'estetica antica* (The power of appearance: A historical-critical survey of ancient aesthetics). Casoria-Naples: Loffredo.

Todorov, Tzvetan. 1984. *Teorie del simbolo* (Theories of the symbol). Milan: Garzanti. Published as *Théories du symbol* (1977).

Trione, Vincenzo. 2019. *L'opera interminabile. Arte e XXI secolo* (The endless work: Art in the twenty-first century). Turin: Einaudi.

Untersteiner, Mario. (1938) 2019. *Il concetto di Daimon in Omero* (The concept of the daemon in Homer). Rome: Aseq.

Valéry, Paul 2015. "Intérieur." In *Collected Works of Paul Valéry*. Vol. 1. *Poems*. Princeton, NJ: Princeton University Press.

Vasugupta. 2013. *Gli aforismi di Śiva* (The aphorisms of Shiva). Edited by R. Torelli. Milan: Adelphi.

Venturi Ferriolo, Massimo. 2019. *Oltre il giardino. Filosofia del paesaggio* (Beyond the garden: A philosophy of the landscape). Turin: Einaudi.

Vercellone, Federico. 2013. *Dopo la morte dell'arte* (After the end of art). Bologna: Il Mulino.

Vischer, Friedrich Theodor. 1989. *Simbolo e forma* (Symbol and form). Milan: Aragno.

– 1997. "Il simbolo" (The symbol). In *Estetica e empatia* (Aesthetics and empathy), edited by Andrea Pinotti, 141–6. Milan: Guerini.

Vitiello, Vincenzo. 2008. *Oblio e memoria del sacro* (Forgetting and remembering the sacred). Bergamo: Moretti e Vitale.

Vitruvius, Marius Pollio. 1990. *De architectura* (On architecture). Pordenone: Studio Tesi.

Voegelin, Eric. 1956–87. *Order and History.* 5 vols. In *The Collected Works of Eric Voegelin*. Baton Rouge: Louisiana State University Press.

Whitehead, Alfred North. 1965. *Processo e realtà*. Milan: Bompiani. Published as *Process and Reality* (1929).

Winkelmann, Johann J. 1980. *Il bello nell'arte. Scritti sull'arte antica (1755–1765)* (The beautiful in art: Essays on ancient art, 1755–65). Edited by Federico Pfister. Turin: Einaudi.

Wittgenstein, Ludwig. 1997. *Tractatus logico-philosophicus e Quaderni 1914–1916* (*Tractatus* and notebooks, 1914–16). Turin: Einaudi.

Wolfflin, Heinrich. 2017. *Rinascimento e Barocco*. Turin: Einaudi. Published as *Renaissance and Baroque* (1888).

Wordsworth, William 1993. *The Prelude*. Oxford: Woodstock Books.

Wunenburger, Jean-Jacques. 1999. *Filosofia delle immagini* (A philosophy of images). Turin: Einaudi.

– 2013. *Lo specchio delle immagini. Gerarchia e traduzione delle rappresentazioni in Platone* (The mirror of images. Hierarchy and the translation of representations in Plato). In *Ekphrasis*, monographic special issue of *Estetica. Studi e ricerche* 1, no. 1, edited by S. Marino and Antonio Stavru.

Xenophon. 1989. *Memorabilia*. Edited by A. Santonio. Milan: Rizzoli.

Zecchi, Stefano. 1990. *La bellezza* (On beauty). Turin: Bollàti Boringhieri.

Zarlino, Gioseffo. 1562. *Le istituzioni harmoniche* (Rules of harmony). Venice: Francesco Senese.

Zolla, Elémire. 1959. *Eclissi dell'intellettuale* (Eclipse of the intellectual). Milan: Bompiani.

– 1992. *Uscite dal mondo* (Ways out of the world). Milan: Adelphi.

– (1971) 1998. *Che cos'è la tradizione?* (What is tradition?). Milan: Adelphi.

Index